IN HIS OWN WORDS

Dave

I hope you find this interesting and enjoyable. I had eight years working for and with Harold Hughes.

Bill

Harold Hughes was a political giant who rose from truck driver to member and chairman of the Iowa State Commerce Commission (1958–1962), to Governor of Iowa (1962–1968), and eventually to U.S. Senator (1969–75). He was considered by many, qualified for the presidency. Photo: Governor Harold E. Hughes, State Historical Society of Iowa, Des Moines.

IN HIS OWN WORDS

Alcoholic | Truck Driver | Governor | US Senator

The Harold Hughes Story

RUSSELL WILSON & WILLIAM HEDLUND

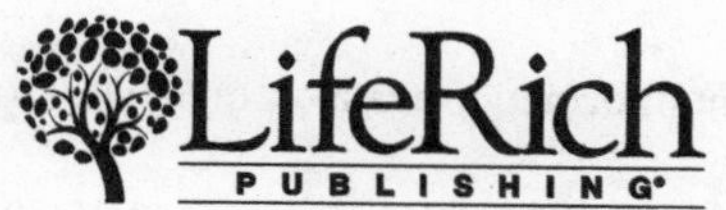

Copyright © 2020 Russell Wilson & William Hedlund.

All rights reserved. No part of this book may be used or reproduced by any means, graphic, electronic, or mechanical, including photocopying, recording, taping or by any information storage retrieval system without the written permission of the author except in the case of brief quotations embodied in critical articles and reviews.

LifeRich Publishing is a registered trademark of The Reader's Digest Association, Inc.

LifeRich Publishing books may be ordered through booksellers or by contacting:

LifeRich Publishing
1663 Liberty Drive
Bloomington, IN 47403
www.liferichpublishing.com
844-686-9607

Because of the dynamic nature of the Internet, any web addresses or links contained in this book may have changed since publication and may no longer be valid. The views expressed in this work are solely those of the author and do not necessarily reflect the views of the publisher, and the publisher hereby disclaims any responsibility for them.

Any people depicted in stock imagery provided by Getty Images are models, and such images are being used for illustrative purposes only.
Certain stock imagery © Getty Images.

Cover design by Connie Wilson

Cover photo: A relaxed Harold Hughes in 1963 during a fishing trip in the Yellow River Forest in Northeast Iowa. Fishing was a favorite pastime throughout his life. Personal photo used with permission of the Hughes family.

ISBN: 978-1-4897-3102-9 (sc)
ISBN: 978-1-4897-3101-2 (hc)
ISBN: 978-1-4897-3103-6 (e)

Library of Congress Control Number: 2020917948

Print information available on the last page.

LifeRich Publishing rev. date: 10/15/2020

CONTENTS

(Left to right) Friend and longtime Hughes supporter William Knapp, Governor Harold Hughes, Hughes' daughter Phyllis, and wife Eva, with the author, Russell Wilson at Knapp's Sugar Creek Farm, west of Des Moines in 1966. Photo: Personal photo used with permission of William Knapp.

FOREWORD

I am pleased and honored to write the foreword for this book. I knew Harold E. Hughes for many years. I considered him one of my closest friends. I also considered him to have been the most effective governor in Iowa's history.

The two men who have written the book are eminently qualified to write the book.

Russell (Russ) Wilson was a close friend of Hughes, or "Pack" as he knew him. Russell was a student pastor at a church in Ida Grove, Iowa, Hughes' hometown, where they became close friends. When Hughes was governor, he appointed Russ to the Iowa Board of Control of State Institutions. During this time, Russ often traveled with Hughes and directed several major projects for the governor, including authoring the Iowa Comprehensive Alcoholism Project.

William (Bill) Hedlund was one of Hughes' top aides as governor and as U.S. Senator. Bill handled many major programs and presentations for the governor. He also played an important role in the administration of the Senator's office in Washington, D.C.

These two men possess a rich mine of experiences with Hughes, both personal and professional. And, I believe they have done an excellent job of sharing their, and many others', experience with this extraordinary man.

WILLIAM KNAPP

"It is essential that we dream great dreams, lay out long-range plans, and take bold action."
Harold E. Hughes from a gubernatorial campaign speech.
Photo: Harold Hughes, State Historical Society of Iowa, Des Moines.

INTRODUCTION

Harold Hughes was a giant of a man. He was a physical giant who stood six feet three inches and weighed some two hundred and thirty five pounds.

He was a political giant who rose from truck driver to member and Chairman of the Iowa Commerce Commission (1958–1962), to Governor of Iowa (1962–1968), and eventually to U.S. Senator (1969–75).

He was a spiritual giant who embraced the Christian faith throughout his career and eventually retired from the Senate to devote his time to full-time lay ministry.

Hughes overcame many formidable obstacles in his life. He grew up in abject poverty, often hunting, fishing, and trapping to provide food for his family.

The authors and members of Hughes' family believe that a former autobiography does not give him adequate credit for his highly productive life. This book is not intended to be another biography of Harold E. Hughes. Nor is it intended to be an academic work. It is intended to reveal the many facets of Hughes' colorful, tragic, complex, successful, productive, and spiritual life from the perspective of people who knew him best. It's also meant to give him well-deserved credit for the huge impact he made on the lives of thousands of alcoholics and other people in this country.

When the authors began the research for the book they were surprised and delighted to learn that Julianne, Harold's second wife, had collected many photos and articles about him. Among those items were many hours of recordings made by the senator in anticipation of his writing a second book. Those recordings are a rich mine of information about him and many are included in this book in his own words.

These are troublesome days in U.S. politics, when the rating of Congress is the lowest in history, when 'gridlock' describes the paralysis that pervades the Congress and makes it nearly impossible for it to address the nation's pressing problems. Statesmanship is in short supply. In these times, Hughes' story is a refreshing reminder of how politics can be, and hopefully will be, again.

A 1996 quote in *The Des Moines Register* by James Flansburg embodies the authors' intent best — "I am trying to explain the man who — substantially more than anyone else — remade and recast the American political system and, before that, Iowa state and local government."[1]

It is our hope that Hughes' story, his philosophy and practice of government, and his depth of character will be an inspiration to all politicians, and especially the young who are aspiring to enter public life.

Notes

1 Flansburg, James, "Hughes' Faith in Democracy," *Des Moines Register*, November 3, 1996.

Photo: A relaxed Harold Hughes in 1963 during a fishing trip in the Yellow River Forest in Northeast Iowa. Fishing was a favorite pastime throughout his life. Photo: Personal photo used with permission of the Hughes family.

A devout Christian, Harold Hughes pulled himself out of a life of drinking to become the thirty-sixth governor of the State of Iowa. Shown here with his wife, Eva, daughter, Phyllis, and dog, Mike, in the governor's mansion, Christmas circa 1966-67.
Photo: Official state photo used for Christmas card

CHAPTER ONE

Hour of Despair

I prayed for the first time without any guile. I prayed, 'God help me because I can't help myself.' It suddenly happened that my heart was strangely warmed. I can't explain it, but God touched my life.

HAROLD E. HUGHES

Hughes began drinking in his youth and continued into adulthood. He continued to drink in the Army and for several years after his discharge. In January of 1954, feeling helpless to the grip of alcohol and ashamed of the way his life was going, he came to an hour of despair. This is his account, in his own words:

"For some time, I sat in the car in our driveway not wanting to get out. A cold, January night wind moaned through the bare trees. The house looming before me was dark, and I sensed it was as empty as my soul.

"I felt sure my wife and little daughters were gone. Eva had often left when she thought I'd be coming home drunk. Finally, I climbed out of the car and carefully made my way to the house. A tricycle clattered along the sidewalk when I banged into it, but I didn't sense any pain. Reaching the steps, I stood there for a moment holding on to a rounded porch column.

"Dimly, I remembered kissing Eva goodbye this morning. She had reminded me of tonight's dinner invitation. We had a limited social life because of my drinking, and this evening was very important to her. As I drove away, I had looked back to see Eva still standing on the porch. She looked so sad. I reminded myself to bring her some flowers.

"It had been a busy day. I ran a small association of motor-truck drivers in Iowa and that afternoon had met with some shippers over a knotty problem. Finally when all was settled, one of the men suggested that we retire to a bar to confirm our decision.

"I hesitated. I had not taken a drink the past two weeks. Something told me to go straight home. But then, why not just sit at the bar for a moment? Besides, hadn't I learned control?

"Just one drink, I thought. That would be it. One drink and I'd say good-bye. I glanced at my watch. I still had time.

"The bourbon tasted good, and I relaxed in the pleasant warmth of it. Later, through a murky maroon fog, I heard someone say something about it being eleven o'clock.

"Eleven o'clock!

"I hurried to my car in the parking lot, where the cold night air cleared my head, and I drove home.

"Eva, I called hoarsely as I pushed open the front door. But my voice echoed hollowly in the hall. I was sure she had taken Connie and Carol to her mother's.

"I stumbled and fell to a couch, breathing heavily. Cold sweat beaded my forehead as hopelessness overwhelmed me. I remembered how long Eva had sewn material to make a new dress for the dinner tonight. Again, I had hurt the ones I loved so much."

Hughes continues, "Now, as I lay on the couch in my empty house, my head pounded with guilt and nausea. How many times had I sworn off drinking, promising Eva that I wouldn't touch another drop? How many times had I failed?

"The sense of shame sank deeper into me as I lay there. I felt helpless. A father in his thirties who was worthless, a sot. What was the point in going on any longer? I thought of how Eva's once lively brown eyes had dulled and worry lines etched her face. Though I never struck her, I'd come home belligerent and foulmouthed. And she would cringe like a beaten kitten. One night Connie and Carol were awakened by my shouting, and I almost stumbled over them at the top of the stairs where they lay huddled, crying.

"A drumbeat of doom seemed to fill my days and nights. I cringed at the knowing winks by other people, at seeing the flush in my face in the mirror, at the deepening fatigue that racked my body. Yet I was powerless to stop doing the one thing that caused it all.

"Trying to escape the horrible self-loathing, I struggled up from the couch and wandered about the empty house. In our bedroom, I slumped onto the bed. I sat there, sunk in an awful despair.

"What was the point of living? I'd failed everyone who had meant anything to me. I was a disgrace to my town. I was a hypocrite in everything I did. I couldn't even tell the truth anymore.

"I couldn't do anything right. Why not just end it? The thought hung there, like the echo of a tolling bell.

"A cold feeling of logic overcame me. Why not? I had thought about this before but had brushed it away. Yet the more I now considered the alternative, the more sense it made. Why go on doing the things I hated? The more I thought about the disorder in my life and the inability to control it, the more I wanted to end it. I was just an evil rotten drunk, a liar. And what should happen to evil men? They deserve to die.

"I remembered enough scripture to know that suicide was not God's way. But as I weighed the balance, I felt it better to be eternally lost than to bring eternal hell to those I loved.

"No, my mind was clear now. I hated what I did. But I still did it. When I promised loved ones I wouldn't drink, and even prayed to God that I wouldn't drink, I did it again and again. I realized in my heart that there was no way on earth I could ever control it.

"I got up from the bed and went to the closet where I kept my rifle and shotgun. I opened the door and considered both, and then reached for the shotgun. It would be most certain. It was a single-barrel, Remington pump gun, a 12-gauge.

"As I lifted the gun into the room, its walnut stock glowed in the bedroom light. The gun had belonged to Jesse, my brother, killed in an accident some years ago. He had been so proud of it. I thought about Jesse. Then I considered what I was going to do to Mother, Dad, Eva, and the children. Eva was still young and beautiful. She would easily find someone else and have a decent life. The thought hurt me.

The girls would eventually forget me. As I was now, they could never forget, suffering only disgrace and sorrow.

"I thought about insurance. I had let my G.I. insurance lapse, but I did have a benevolence society policy that would pay my burial expenses.

"I slid three shells into the magazine and pumped one into the chamber. Tears streaming down my face, I lay down on the bed, rested the shotgun on my chest, and put the muzzle into my mouth. The cold steel rasped my teeth and tasted of oil. Reaching down, I found I could push the trigger with my thumb. This way everything was certain. I did not want to botch it and spend the rest of my life as a vegetable.

"Then I thought of the awful mess this would leave in the bedroom. I remembered the men I had seen shot overseas. I was leaving Eva and the girls with enough memories. Getting up, I walked through the hall and into the bathroom. It could be cleaned easier. Carefully holding the Remington, I climbed into the old-fashioned claw-footed tub, my shoe soles squeaking on the bottom. In it, I lay down, feeling strange to be there with my clothes on. With the shotgun resting on my stomach, I positioned it with the muzzle in my mouth toward my brain. Reaching down, my thumb found the trigger — and I was about to push it.

"A terrible sadness filled me. I knew what I was doing was wrong in God's eyes. Yet my whole life had been wrong. And God had always been very remote. In a few years my family would get over it, I reasoned. They would have an opportunity to rebuild their lives. But if I remained here, I would never change and only hurt them more. The thought came that I should explain all this to God before pushing the trigger. Then if He could not forgive this sin, at least He would know exactly why I was committing it.

"Climbing out of the tub, I knelt on the tile floor and laid my head on my arms, resting on the cool tub rim.

'Oh, God,' I groaned, 'I'm a failure, a drunk, a liar, and a cheat. I'm lost and hopeless and want to die. Forgive me for doing this … ' I broke into sobs. 'Oh, Father, please take care of Eva and the girls.

Please help them forget me …' I slid to the floor, convulsing in heavy sobbing. As I lay down on the tiles, crying and trying to talk to God, my throat swelled until I couldn't utter a sound. Totally exhausted, I lay silent, drained, and still.

"I do not know how long I lay there. But in the quiet bathroom, a strange peace gently settled over me. Something I had never experienced before was happening, something far beyond my senseless struggles. A warm peace seemed to settle deep within me, filling the terrible emptiness, driving out the self-hate and condemnation. My sins seemed to evaporate like moisture spots under a hot, bright sun.

"God was reaching down and touching me. A God who cared. A God who loved me. A God who was concerned for me despite my sins. Like a stricken child lost in a storm, I had suddenly stumbled into the warm arms of my Father. Joy filled me — so intense it seemed to burst my breast. Slowly I rose to my knees and looked up to Him in awe and gratitude. Kneeling on that bathroom floor, I gave myself to him totally, 'Whatever You ask me to do, Father,' I cried through hot tears, 'I will do it.'

"For a long time I knelt there. Then I stood up, breathing heavily as if I had just climbed a long hill. Reaching into the tub, I picked up the shotgun. I shuddered as I thought how close I had come to using it. Taking it to our bedroom, I unloaded the shells and placed the gun back in the closet. As I closed the closet door, a faint accusatory echo sounded: 'Coward … afraid to pull the trigger.'

"Doubt chilled me. Had my experience in the bathroom been another of the many illusions I had gone through before? I was so deceitful to myself and others. But something far stronger kept saying: 'Stay with God. Follow Him. Believe.'

"I knelt at the bed: 'Father', I prayed, 'I don't understand this or know why I deserve it. For You know how weak I am. But I put myself in Your hands. Please give my family back to me … and give me the strength never to run again. Father, I put myself in Your hands.'

"I finally climbed into bed, resting my head on the pillow, and for the first time in months, slipped into a deep, peaceful sleep.

"Bright sunshine streaming through the window awakened me. Exuberance filled me, and then I remembered the night before. I got up and made coffee, thinking how close I had come to killing myself. I knew that if I drank again I would put myself under the control of the dark forces that would lead me to the same horrible pit.

"But I also knew I had Someone with me, a personal Being who had reached down in my desperation and comforted me. As I thought of Him, again that strange joy filled me."[1]

Notes

1 Hughes, Harold with Schneider, Dick, *The Man From Ida Grove,* Chosen Books Publishing Company, Ltd., Lincoln, VA, 1978.

Harold Hughes never forgot his humble beginnings and treasured the simple things in life. A dedicated family man, he is shown here with daughters (from left) Phyllis, Carol, and Connie, singing around the piano in the governor's mansion in 1963.
Photo: Personal family photo used with permission of the Hughes family.

Senator Hughes shares memories with 81-year-old Sally Ison, his mother Etta Hughes' sister, and her family in February 1973.
Photo: Personal family photo used with permission of the Hughes family.

CHAPTER TWO

Pulaski County, Kentucky

I was born in a hospital in Ida Grove, Iowa, which was an old frame house just three-fourths of a block from the Baxter Hotel. The house still stands in Ida Grove. Dad had borrowed money to put in a crop and buy feed for the hogs and sows, and everything burned up. That ended farming.

HAROLD E. HUGHES

It was a bitter, cold day on February 10, 1922. Etta Kelley Hughes was in the hospital in Ida Grove, Iowa, delivering a baby. That baby boy weighed barely five pounds and was named Harold Everett Hughes. Little did his father, Lewis, and his mother, Etta, know until later that the farmhouse and barn that they had rented on land they planned to farm had burned to the ground. Everything they owned was destroyed including machinery and horses, which in those days were absolutely essential for farming.

A relative of Hughes wrote in a paper about the lineage of Harold E. Hughes, "By word of mouth from generation to generation the people in this account originally came from the rugged country of Wales. They were an adventurous people named Hughes, sometimes spelled Hewes. They came to the new world when it was still wilderness. Some of them fought in the Revolutionary War, and all had a small part in the beginnings of the American Republic. They settled in the Carolinas, looking for greener pastures, then followed the trend to go westward. When they reached the rich, virgin timbered hills of Pulaski County, Kentucky, watered by the Cumberland River and Pitman Creek, they were content."[1]

Jacob Hughes, Hughes' grandfather, was one of a third generation in his family to settle in Pulaski County, Kentucky. Jacob and his wife, Lydia, lived on a farm in Cabin Hollow. Jacob supplemented his means by working for the Kentucky Lumber Company at Burnside.

Jacob was a strong man physically and spiritually. According to the family story, Jacob carried a barrel of flour on his shoulders from Burnside to Cabin Hollow, a distance of approximately six miles. He was a God-fearing man, and he and Lydia were active members of the Pumpkin Hollow Baptist Zion Church. They had two sons, Lewis and Oscar.

According to Phyllis Hughes Ewing, Hughes' youngest daughter, "The first Hughes to come to Ida County were Harold's father, Lewis, and his father, Jacob. Jacob was one of eighteen children. One by one, the Hughes came to Ida County. My grandmother, Etta, was twenty-six or twenty-seven years old when she was married. She had been engaged to another young man who died of tuberculosis before they could get married, and she vowed she would never marry. She kept her vow for several years, and then she and my grandfather got together and married. They decided to try and follow Cousin Norman to Iowa. They got as far as Bloomington, Illinois, and their car broke down. Their money ran out and they ended up working there for five years."

Hughes recalled, "I was born in a hospital in Ida Grove which was an old frame home just three-fourths of a block from the Baxter Hotel. The house still stands there in Ida Grove. Dad had borrowed money to put in a crop and buy feed for the hogs and sows, and everything burned up. That ended farming. There was nothing my dad could do but hire out as a farm hand. He worked for Mr. Page. We had an old farmhouse to live in.

"I was born with jaundice. We had gone through a bad year on the farm without a great deal to eat, certainly not the nutrition my mother and I needed. As a result of that, when I was born I weighed less than five pounds and had jaundice, and, as the doctor told my mother, I 'wasn't much to look at.' She got pretty upset by that. But I guess I wasn't, you know.

"[My brother] Jess was almost three years older than I. He would have been three on March 10. I was born on February 10, and he was two years and eleven months older than I was. At the time the only two crops that there was a market for were pumpkins and watermelons. Dad fed most of the pumpkins to the hogs. He took the watermelons to town and sold them on the street corner out of a wagon box. That was about 1922."

Phyllis continues, "In his later life, Dad planned to publish another book of his life and recorded a history of his family." That material was never published, but fortunately the family shared the material with the authors of this book. In the recording, Hughes shared the following memories of his mother.

"Mother was a strong-willed woman and a very strong physical woman until, I'd say, the 1940's. My memory of her as a boy was that she was a big woman, heavy-set, with dark red hair. My brother inherited her red hair. I took after my father's side of the family in appearance. My mother was always happy. She often played jokes on people and sang a lot. I remember as a boy growing up hearing her singing hymns in the kitchen as she worked and playing jokes on people. She had a lot of life and a lot of energy, and she was a very religious woman. Her church and her family meant a great deal to her."

Hughes recalls his grandmother. "Again, this is family talk. My grandmother on my mother's side of the family had the physical appearance of an Indian. If you saw a picture of her, you would see her high cheekbones, long, black, straight hair — my maternal grandmother. The family rumors had it that she was one-quarter Cherokee Indian. I don't know that for sure. I've never made any effort to trace that down. She was teaching school in St. Joseph, Missouri when my grandfather met her and took her back to Kentucky where they got married.

"Most of my mother's family went through school. My mother had the poorest education in the whole family. One of her sisters was a teacher, and the other was a nurse. They went to what was then a normal training school that was the state educational system for boarding schools. You went away from home to board and go to school. Mother stayed home and worked and did not go to that school. As a result, she never had the benefits of education the way the other members of the family did."

Hughes continues, "I found out when I was older that she had had a complete hysterectomy. At that period in life we were alone for quite a period of time when my mother was gone to Iowa City to the hospital. We couldn't get treatment for that kind of surgery at home because we didn't have any money. They hauled Mother off to Iowa City. They went by train to Cedar Rapids. Then they took a little commuter down to Iowa City. It was a long session, that kind of surgery. They came back the same way. You went alone. No one went with you. They didn't have road ambulances in those days. It was a long trip. We 'batched' it out and got along all right when Mother was away. We used to wonder about it you know. I remember as a child saying goodbye to Dad as he left for the hospital.

"My dad was of a serious nature, and he had a lot of illness in his life. He had trouble with stomach ulcers for a long period of years. In fact, when I was thirteen years old, my father started hemorrhaging ... and I can remember they wouldn't let him in the hospital in Ida Grove because we didn't have the money. We got three doctors over to the house, and they all reached the same conclusion — that he wouldn't live. Finally, we got him into a hospital in Sioux City. He did live, but again, it was one of those cases where if you didn't have the money, you didn't get help. I've never forgotten those times because not having money to get what you need happened to me several times in my life.

"I look much like my grandfather on my father's side. My grandfather was a big man, and my father was a big man. But neither one was physically as big as I am. Actually, Jesse was bigger than I was. He was named Big Pack for pachyderm, and I was named Little Pack for little pachyderm. My grandfather had a reputation in his early years in and around Burnside, Kentucky, of being one of the strongest men that had ever been around there. He was physically one of the most powerful men, I think, that has ever lived. He was just plain physically powerful. He died, I believe, in 1955. I never heard my grandfather say a swear word. My grandfather was also one of the best cooks that ever lived. In his early life, he had cooked in a lumber camp and was a lumberjack down in the mountains. My father and my uncle used to cut wagon spokes. They also cut railroad ties. They'd camp out in the winter and cut railroad ties. They had to meet a certain specification. They'd create rafts up along the river and wait for the spring flood. When the flood came, they rode the rafts down the river to the point where they could sell them.

"We had a good doctor in Ida Grove, old Dr. Morehead, who treated our family and gave us medical care all of our lives. The last I remember of Dr. Morehead, he was in his nineties and still practicing medicine. He wrote a beautiful history of Ida County in which I was deeply interested. He was my doctor all of my life, and we seldom ever paid him in full. We were just constantly in debt with Dr. Morehead. He never charged much. He used old-fashioned remedies. I suppose most people have forgotten white iodine for tonsillitis and sore throats and the herbs and potions for other illnesses."

Hughes recorded, "When I was a little boy, there was an epidemic of diphtheria, and I got it. They gave me a spinal injection. It was one of the most horrible experiences of my life. I also had the mumps and measles. My brother had scarlet fever, but I didn't get it. We got whooping cough on the way to Kentucky in the Model T. I contracted the mumps and damned near died."

Hughes recalls a tragic accident when he was a toddler. "The reason I remember this experience is that it involved a great deal of pain. When I was a young child, I remember standing on a chair before an open kitchen cook range watching my mother cooking. She turned around, and I turned around and fell with my hands on top of the stove. And, of course, I very severely burned my hands. I started screaming. I can remember the severe pain and my mother crying. I also burned my elbows and my stomach as I rolled off the stove. I can remember that because it was in the middle of the winter, and we lived in the middle of what was known as the Page Farm.

"At that time, a severe snowstorm was in process. There was no way to get to a doctor or to get a doctor there right away. As a result, for a long time I just endured the pain with the home remedies that we had. I can remember several days of just pure agony. I can remember a long period of time with mother and father both just walking the floor with me and trying to relieve the pain as best as they could. They glopped butter and lard on me at the same time.

"I also remember the first time in my life that I had pneumonia. I've had pneumonia several times, but this time we were unable to get a doctor because we were snowed in. We were living out on the farm. As a result of that I went through the critical periods of high temperature and wondering whether I would live or not. Those are probably two of the earliest points in my memory. I can recall fragments of days on that farm and in that farmhouse. I can still recall the appearance of the kitchen because my mother used to put a blanket down so I could crawl around. That was a long time, until the time that the family went back to Kentucky. When we went to Kentucky, I was only three years old. So, I am talking about the latter months of the first years of my life."

Hughes continued, "There was a depression in 1922 that nearly everyone has forgotten about. Nonetheless, it was a very severe depression. Dad was farming at that time. In the migration from Kentucky, he and Mother had gone to McLean County, Illinois and lived for five years and had farmed there. Dad worked as a farm hand. Then he came to Ida County and worked on a number of farms as a farm hand. He tried to start farming when I was born, but that ended in disaster when everything burned down.

"Then my grandmother [my mother's mother], who had been ill with cancer, was progressively getting worse. As a result, my parents made the decision to go back to Kentucky to take care of my grandmother. Her illness was terminal, and they knew it. It was just a question of time. I can remember quite a bit about being there. I can remember sitting on the bed with my grandmother when they would bring lunch and dinner in to her. She used to feed me a little something off of her tray.

"My grandmother died and we went from there to Poor Fork, Kentucky, where my father went into a business venture with my uncle, my mother's sister's husband, Mr. Ison. It was a little grocery store venture. Dad sold groceries and commodities out of a little old truck that he drove around to the neighboring mining towns delivering door-to-door."

Hughes recalls, "My brother, Jesse, was born in Strawberry, Kentucky, which was a post office address. I can remember traveling those towns with my father and my mother. I remember an incident where we knocked at a door in one of those places. My mother was selling those California Perfume Goods, and a voice said, 'Come in.' We went in, There was no one in the house but this great big parrot sitting in a cage that had said 'come in.' Of course, about that time, the lady came home and we were in the house. We explained to her that the parrot had invited us in. She just laughed about it. The parrot always hollered 'come in' any time someone knocked on the door. While she and mother were talking, I stuck my finger in the cage, and that big old parrot just about tore it off! I'll never forget that incident. Again, an incident of pain, you know, something that sharpens your memory, I guess.

"I have memories of being with my father when he was traveling the grocery route. We used to stop at one of these boarding houses for lunch where people all sat down at a common table, and the food was all on the table. You helped yourself. This was between the times that I was three and five years old. Those were incidents and memories that I can pick up and remember during that period of time."

Phyllis, Harold's daughter, recalled an incident involving her grandmother, Etta Hughes, who remained in Kentucky. Etta grew up in Kentucky with men who were hunters, trappers and fishermen. No doubt she learned to shoot and handle a gun as a young girl. Phyllis recalls her father telling this story:

"When my grandparents, Lewis and Etta, returned to Kentucky from Ida Grove to care for my grandmother who was dying of cancer, they remained in Kentucky for several months. During that time my father joined a grocery business with my mother Etta's sister's husband, Mr. Ison. Occasionally my dad loaded a Model T pick-up truck and traveled into the mountains and sold groceries house to house to the people there.

"When my grandfather made those grocery runs, that meant leaving my grandmother at home alone with the boys. Concerned for her safety while alone, my grandfather advised my grandmother that if anyone threatened her, she should shoot them.

"Sure enough, one night late an intruder came to the cabin and tried to gain entry by pounding on the locked door. My grandmother warned the intruder. When he continued to attempt to gain entry, she shot through the door.

"My grandmother didn't sleep the rest of the night. In the morning she opened the door. There were bloodstains on the ground and a trail of blood down the lane but no body. She had no further problems with unwanted intruders."

"We had an old Model T Ford at one time," Hughes recalls." We made the trip from Ida Grove, Iowa, to Somerset, Kentucky, in that car. I can remember parts of the trip. There were dirt roads much of the time and sometimes we had to drive through a mud hole and would get stuck. There would be a farmer sitting there with a big team of horses. He would pull us through for fifty cents and we didn't have much money. It took us two weeks to make that trip from Ida Grove, Iowa, to Somerset, Kentucky, in that Model T. Ford. I have driven it many times since in just a day.

"The move back to Iowa was triggered by economic circumstances and the desire of my mother and father to get my brother and me to where we could get a decent education. The quality of educational opportunities back in the mountains in Eastern Kentucky at that time was not very good. My brother was due to start school the next year. Mother and Father both felt strongly that if there was one thing we boys had to have, it was a high school education. Neither one of them had had the benefit of that, and they felt strongly about it.

"My mother was separated from her family from the time I came on this earth. She never lived in proximity to her family. When her father died, we were too poor to afford to even send Mother down there for the funeral. We didn't have the money. There was no way she could get there, so she didn't get to the funeral for her father. When her mother died, of course, we were there. But, after that, it was a long, long period of time before my mother got to see any of her brothers and sisters."

Notes

1 Hughes, Esther Louise, *The Heritage of a Governor*, a paper.

Lewis and Etta Hughes, Harold Hughes' parents, in Ida Grove, Iowa.
Photo: Personal family photo used with permission of the Hughes family.

CHAPTER THREE

Growing Up on the Farm

"I sang in the chorus. I sang in the Boys Glee Club and in the boy's quartet. I played in a madrigal group and in the high school band. I played the tuba solo. I also sang a baritone voice solo. I was involved in everything. It took every minute of time I had to do those things during school time with groups and usually during study periods."

HAROLD E. HUGHES

While reading the Hughes story, a few themes emerge. One of the obvious themes throughout his childhood and youth is poverty. Although as a child Harold didn't seem to suffer, poverty, no doubt, made an indelible impression on him, and it also affected his first wife, Eva.

Prior to Harold's birth, his mother and father lived in the mountains in Pulaski County, Kentucky, where making even a marginal living was a daily challenge. His father had some formal education; his mother had none and no marketable skills. They made the decision to move to Iowa where they had relatives.

Their migratory trip to Iowa was delayed by a breakdown of their car in Bloomington, Illinois, and the end of their meager savings. After five hard-working years, they arrived in Ida Grove only to have their rented farmhouse and their equipment and livestock destroyed by fire. Determined to survive, they picked themselves up and started again. Harold's father worked as a farmhand and at construction labor for many years at minimal salaries.

During their first few years in Ida Grove, Harold's father had a serious illness and was near death. They could not get him into the local hospital because there was no money. Later, when his mother needed surgery, she made the long and arduous journey alone to a hospital in Iowa City, approximately two hundred and fifty miles away, where she could get treatment for free. She left the family behind to fend for themselves.

Harold and his brother, Jesse, each had only one pair of overalls to wear to school and one outfit to wear on Sunday. "Well, 'we can't afford it' was a common byword with us. We used to go through the catalog figuring out what we could afford to buy on this year's order for school. If I could get one new pair of overalls and two new shirts, I thought I was really in good shape and, I was proud. The Hughes maintained a large garden and Etta sometimes canned as much as six hundred quarts of vegetables and fruit each year. They would have starved if they had not raised chickens, hunted wild game, and fished.

Eva, Hughes' first wife, and her family grew up in even more dire circumstances. Her father died very young leaving her mother to provide for Eva and three siblings. There were no financial safety nets, no Social Security, no social welfare. In those days there was not even a community food bank in Holstein, Iowa, where they lived.

In their early days of marriage, Harold and Eva lived under the poverty line. The economic depressions in 1922 and 1929 made jobs scarce and wages at poverty levels. When they first moved to Des Moines, they barely survived for two weeks on a sack of potatoes that Harold had managed to purchase.

Living in poverty and need no doubt influenced Hughes' later identification with small individual truckers and his fight for fair tariffs. Those experiences probably caused him to also fight for alcoholics who were unemployed and their families suffering from deprivation. Those experiences must have also motivated him to persuade the Iowa Legislature to increase the poverty-level salaries of attendants in the state's mental hospitals, and guards and other staff in the state's prisons. Harold was sensitive to the needs and struggles of the poor, disenfranchised, and marginalized his entire career.

When Hughes was thirteen or fourteen, he and his brother, Jesse, did what they could to provide for the family. At one point their father was ill for several months and unable to work for a year. The boys worked in construction and as farm hands baling hay, shocking oats, and doing whatever they could to earn money. They picked up junk, old copper kettle ware, and aluminum pots and pans, which they could sell for a few cents a pound.

Their father salvaged a pair of old sled runners from the city dump and made a platform for a sled. Hughes recalls, "It was one of the fastest sleds in town. I was prouder of that sled than anything I ever had."[1]

Hughes continues, "I remember both Jesse and I wanted to join the Civilian Conservation Corps, the CCC camps, because my father was unable to work for almost a year when he had this stomach trouble and hemorrhages. As a result of that, Jesse felt he had to help support the family. We both wanted to go to a CCC camp, but mother wouldn't let us. Jesse was able to get part-time work as a construction worker on weekends and in the summertime. Jesse and I both worked as construction workers. We did everything working on the farms for fifty cents a day and lunch. Sometimes we were lucky and got one dollar a day for farm work."[2]

Hughes reminisces, "We caddied on the golf course and hunted golf balls. One day I was caddying an old guy who knocked two golf balls in the creek and wanted me to go get them. Well, I took off my clothes and went in the creek and got them out. He offered me a nickel a piece for them. I threw them back in the creek again. He got upset and tried to have me banned from the golf course for being insubordinate to a member. The other guys playing with him laughed at him so hard. They wouldn't let him. I didn't go back and get his golf balls again for a nickel. That had been a lot of work and a lot of risk, fishing around in an old dirty creek trying to find two new golf balls, but that was basically the type of youth we had.

"We did a lot of hunting, a lot of fishing, a lot of trapping, and a lot of working in the garden. We did the routine playing that kids do while we were growing up. We didn't have the things that kids have nowadays and a lot of things that I guess other kids had then, but I wasn't aware of them."[3]

Parenthetically, Hughes' daughter, Phyllis, later recalled, "My father inherited the outdoor ethic from his father and grandfather who grew up in Kentucky. Hunting, trapping, and fishing provided essential food, clothing, and income for the family. When there was no work to gain income the women would plant big gardens, and the men would hunt and fish. It was part of their DNA, and my father inherited some of those genes."

Phyllis continues, "I started walking the trapline with my father when I was about three years old over my mother's protest, but Dad would take me with him. We'd be out at dawn walking the trapline. Then I grew up to be a ferocious animal rights advocate and lifelong vegetarian. My two sisters came along when my folks were first married. I came along nine to ten years later, unexpected. I think my dad thought he was going to get a son to pass along all the hunting and fishing skills, and then he got a vegetarian, animal rights activist daughter.[4]

"I sat out in the duck and goose blinds with him. We went fishing every weekend to Black Hawk Lake in Lake View. That was our home away from home. That outdoor ethic of his, being out there, was his lifeline. That's what he wanted to do more than anything."[5]

Hughes continues, "We never owned a bicycle. We couldn't afford a bicycle and I never asked for one. I didn't want to be asking my parents for things that I knew we couldn't afford to buy. At one time we had two scooters and two pairs of roller skates. I can remember those because when one scooter finally wore out, we built one out of the two. We still had one scooter between us, which was a pretty proud thing for us in those days. I don't see scooters anymore, so I guess kids don't use them anymore. But back in those days, it was quite a toy. We used to wheel around on them all over creation.

"I can remember the first gun I ever had, in fact, I've still got it. I bought it with my own money for five dollars and eighty eight cents. It was a 22 rifle, a Winchester 22 single shot rifle. I remember the first time I ever went hunting alone, rabbit hunting. We used to go hunting on Thanksgiving Day for Thanksgiving dinner. We'd go out in the morning and shoot rabbits and pheasants. I'll never forget the first time I went duck hunting and shot a box of shells and came back with two ducks. Dad lectured me for an hour. I'd gone rabbit hunting the Sunday afternoon before and shot a box of shells and got six rabbits. He said, 'with twenty-five shells, you ought to get twenty-five rabbits. There's no sense in missing shots at rabbits, they're the easiest things in the world to hit.' He said, 'I'll go with you, and we'll see what you're doing wrong.' So he did.

"We used to have an old hair-rigger Stevens double-barreled shotgun. If you just went near the trigger, it went off. The first fox I ever shot was when I was 12 years old. I was upset because my dad and brother went out on the trapline and left me at home. I got mad and took that shotgun and walked out over the hill. It was on Christmas morning. I had walked about two miles and came over a little ridge into a valley and there was an old fox lying asleep. He jumped up and looked at me. I looked at him and let him have it. I took the fox home. In those days fox fur was worth a great deal of money. In fact, he brought eleven dollars, I'll never forget. When they came home, I had that fox lying in the middle of the floor. I felt pretty grown up at the time. They didn't have much on the trapline, and I had a fox. It's that sort of thing that made life worth living and a lot of fun.

"Dad, as I remember, was pretty even-tempered. I know I never wanted to get him mad at me because I never forgot the one time he spanked me. It was a pretty rough go, and I didn't want any more of that. Mother was awfully spontaneous, and I didn't want punishment. My mother never had to holler twice. If she said, 'Come here, you're going to get a whipping,' I went. I knew if I didn't go, it would be appealed to a higher source, and my father would take over. I didn't want that at all. I used to march up to my mother and bend over and get my rear whacked. I was always getting into something.

"Both of my parents had a very strong impact on my life. I have looked back on it a number of times. My mother and father were both very strong-willed people, yet they never argued in front of us kids. I can never remember my mother and father having an argument in front of us. I had overheard them a couple of times arguing in the other room, usually about finances or something. They never brought up a family argument in front of us kids. Maybe they did argue, but I was totally unaware of it. They never showed it around us.

"We were treated just about as impartially as two kids could be treated. My brother and I had a great love for each other. We slept together. We had to." Harold recorded the following about his family's poverty. "My grandfather and grandmother had a little money. They could have at times afforded to have helped my father and mother out of some very tight squeezes but didn't. And, they didn't offer any help. Not one dime. They just said it was 'too bad.' My mother went over and cried and begged my grandfather and mother for help. They said 'no.'

"My mother worked scrubbing floors, cleaning houses, cooking and washing dishes in the hotel dining room. She butchered chickens and walked the streets selling them. She didn't have anything to wear to church, but she never complained about it. Maybe she did, you know, but I never heard her complain about it. The only thing I can remember her saying was that there were other people worse off than we were, and we ought to be doing something to help them.

"Usually we were in debt up to our ears. We were behind in the rent, we owed a grocery bill, we owed a doctor bill, and we owed whoever would give us credit. We owed for a little gas for the car and coal oil for the lamps and usually for a little coal at the lumberyard. It was a struggle working all summer so you could get even and get enough credit to get through the next winter. That was our existence. The wolf was always at the door. We didn't have enough money for any frivolities.

"I can remember the incident of winning the raffle for the Christmas tree when I was in the third grade. It was the first Christmas tree we ever had. When they got ready to recess for Christmas vacation, they had a raffle for those of us who didn't have a Christmas tree. I won the raffle. I can remember that we got some cranberries and popcorn and decorated the Christmas tree with pine cones and popcorn and cranberries and the usual things."[6]

Hughes continues, "I wanted to get an education because I felt like I had to have it. I didn't do a lot of extracurricular reading, but what I had to do, I did. And, of course, we never had a radio. In those days radios were not too broadly used anyway. There weren't many of them around. They were expensive and we couldn't afford it."[7]

Hughes remembers school. "I got interested in music when I was in the sixth grade. The band instructor needed a tuba player. He persuaded me to try and learn to play the tuba. There were a lot of teachers that I became very fond of. Some of them are still around. Many of them were still in contact with me. One of them is now in the furniture business in Ida Grove, Joe Dolage, who has been an assistant football coach and a manual training teacher. I had a great deal of difficulty in manual training. Because of that, I thought I'd never get out of school. I made more toothpicks out of two by fours than any kid who ever went through the class.

"I thought they'd have to burn the school down to get rid of me. I couldn't square up a board in six months. I just absolutely had no talent in the manual arts. I made a footstool, but it didn't last long. It fell apart. If it hadn't been for the fact that the teacher was the assistant coach, I doubt if I would have ever gotten through the course.

"I remember, of course, Miss Ferry, who was my fifth grade teacher and had quite an impact on my life. I think she taught about forty-seven years in Ida Grove. She was one of those princesses of teachers who loved children and brought the best out in every child whose life she ever touched. She brought them really to the maximum of their capability and yet was stern about it. I also remember my mathematics teacher whom I always respected. When I was in her class, I was constantly afraid of her, yet she probably taught me more just out of mutual respect and insisting that I could do it.

"I had an inordinate fear of girls in those days. There were no girls in my family and my mother had built into me a religious attitude toward women. That made me feel very distant, very bashful, and afraid to approach girls my own age. I never had a normal dating relationship in school. In fact, I never dated a girl in my own school in all the years I was in high school.

"I was one of the best athletes in the school. I was also one of the best musicians. I suppose by most standards, I was a nice looking, husky young man. But frankly, I never had any money. Most of the time I didn't have enough money to ask someone to go somewhere with me. I was very conscious of that. Plus, I didn't have a car to take anyone anyplace.

"I don't think there was anything that I really enjoyed in the way of subjects of study in school. Everything was hard work for me. Teachers have indicated that I was a good student, but I worked hard to get my lessons. I took books home every night. I was always busy with extra-curricular activities. I sang in the chorus. I sang in the boy's glee club and in the boy's quartet. I played in a madrigal group and in the high school band. I played the tuba solo. I also sang a baritone voice solo. I was involved in everything. It took every minute of time I had to do those things during school time with groups and usually during study periods.

"I used to go to school an hour early in the morning to practice either in band or various groups. I studied at night after I got home, but it was labor for me. I did well in school. I was not exceptional and I was not in the top ten, but I had my share of B's and high C's with the exception of writing. The old Palmer method of penmanship is the only subject I ever failed in school. I must have been one of the worst in the business because I got a red F in that, and I'll never forget it as long as I live.

"Another strange thing. Neither my mother nor my father ever saw me play football. They never went to a track meet. They never heard me play or sing. The reason was they didn't have clothes to wear to those things. They didn't go. In all my life, they never heard me or saw me at a school event."[8]

Notes

1 From recordings made by Harold Hughes in anticipation of his writing a book.
2 Ibid.
3 Ibid.
4 Phyllis Hughes Ewing, Harold Hughes' youngest daughter
5 From recordings made by Harold Hughes in anticipation of his writing a book.
6 Ibid.
7 Ibid.
8 Ibid.

Harold Hughes and Eva with his parents, Lewis and Etta Hughes and their first born, Connie, in Des Moines, shortly before Harold left for the war. At the time, he worked for Des Moines City Parks mowing lawns. Photo: Personal family photo used with permission of the Hughes family.

CHAPTER FOUR

Drinking as a Youth and University Dropout

"Over the summer period my drinking was about the same. I drank, I suppose, every Saturday night. I usually went out on a little spree with three or four other people. I usually wound up drinking too much, but it never got out of control. I had a loss of memory in high school when I got drunk two or three times. Loss of memory has been something that plagued me all the time I drank." [1]

HAROLD E. HUGHES

Hughes recorded: "Well, I think I should talk about the drinking experiences of my life. My father occasionally drank too much. I can remember it as a very little boy. He'd come home drunk. He drove the car in the ditch one time. I remember particularly this sort of thing. My mother raised all kinds of Cain about it. I can remember finding bottles of liquor hid in the outhouse and several places where my dad hid them. He was trying to keep it out of my mother's sight. My mother preached to me from my earliest memory up until right now (laughter) about the evils of liquor and drinking.

"My entire background had been one of a rather strict Methodist non-drinking atmosphere from my mother. Then in the early years of my life, I had the memory of my father drinking too much occasionally with some of his friends and coming home intoxicated. Sometimes he was half-intoxicated and created some family difficulties, mainly in arguments. There was never anything rough. It was just my mother's carrying on about his drinking that made it bad.

"I really never drank that I can remember up until the time I was about fourteen years old. I drank some home brew one day. It was just a glass and I thought it was the awfulest stuff I had ever tasted. I couldn't imagine how in the hell anyone could ever want to drink that crap.

"When I was about fifteen I was running around with boys that were a year or two older than I was. I was big, and you know, I was playing football with all the older kids. I was also involved in athletics with them. When they went out someplace, they drank. So after going with them two or three times and not drinking, I decided, 'Well, hell, I'll drink with them.' I don't even remember what it was that we were drinking, but it was pretty foul stuff. As I've said many times, I never drank normally. The first time I drank, I drank too much. No, it never made me happy. I was never happy when I was drinking.

"I was not like people that seemed to get a glow on and a smile on their face. And then everything is rosy in life when they drink. I don't remember that as being a part of my drinking at all. It was not a happy experience for me. It was sort of a ritualistic experience. I drank, well, psychologically, I drank, to drop my inhibitions because I was a very, as I stated earlier in these recordings, bashful, shy kid. I didn't know what to say to people at the right time and usually said the wrong thing. When I drank, I dropped my inhibitions and I could talk freely.

"I never learned how to dance. Dancing was not encouraged in our home either as were many other things. So when I got to the age when I wanted to date and how to go about it, a drink or two helped me. It helped when I struggled with leaving home and trying to make my way in the world. Drinking also occurred in my life when I started working on construction crews on the road and was constantly with older men. On rainy days they all drank, and it wasn't long before the kid was drinking with the older guys. At that point, some of the men I was working with were twenty-five or thirty. Some of them forty and fifty years old.

"In my high school days, I never drank very often. I didn't like it. It never tasted good to me. I didn't drink for the so-called glow or the high feeling that most people have when they drink. I drank because it dropped all the barriers. I also had a physical addiction when I drank. I never wanted to stop. Some sort of chemical process set up in my body that I wanted to drink three for every drink that someone else drank. I still don't know what it was. It was there. It was there all during the period of my of drinking. Through that period of time, I suppose I got drunk a dozen times. A couple of times I didn't make it home all night. I would worry the hell out of my parents as a result of that. It never interfered with anything. It was just a problem to concern my parents and me. At that point I knew that I wasn't drinking like other people, but I didn't understand why, or know why. I was only seventeen years old.

"I was just to turn eighteen when I graduated. I left home the night I graduated and went to college. I went down to the University of Iowa to work on the campus all summer. I got a job through the athletic department working on construction projects on the campus. I worked as a steamfitter's helper. We were laying new water lines and new steam pipelines in buildings on the campus. I was really a green kid who had never been away from home and never travelled very far. You have to understand; in those days you couldn't afford long journeys and experiences. My range of life's experiences basically in growing up had been in a 150-mile radius of Ida Grove, Iowa. And then I only occasionally got out of town. I went to Chicago on the All-State football team, which was one of the great experiences of my life.

"My drinking in college and on the campus was intermittent. Every couple of weeks we'd go out on a bender. Three or four guys would date a few girls, dance a little, and wind up getting drunk. I didn't drop out of college because of drinking. It has been said that I dropped out of school because of drinking. I just didn't. My drinking didn't really interfere with my education. I worked all summer. I worked all day on construction projects and worked at night in a restaurant washing dishes and scrubbing the floors for the meals that I ate during the day. I was putting in a fifteen-hour day working. Half the money I earned went into a fund for my tuition. In those days they didn't give you tuition grants. At least they didn't to me. When I talk about an athletic scholarship, I'm not talking about them letting me go to school. They just got me a job where I could earn my way through school. That's all they did.

"When school started, I had paid my tuition and had enough money saved back to buy books and the things I needed. Then I got a job, with what I believe was the National Youth Administration (NYA), the national youth program of the time. It was the Roosevelt Era. The job paid twenty dollars a month, which enabled me to pay my room rent, which was ten dollars a month. Three of us lived in one room with three little beds and three little desks and one closet. That left ten dollars a month to pay for things like laundry. I got home about twice during the year and that was the extent of it. I hitchhiked or caught a ride with someone. I couldn't afford to buy a bus ticket.

"In the summer I took on the job of manager and chief lifeguard at the swimming pool in Ida Grove. That was the period when I started dating my future wife. I dated her the first time when I was home in the winter for Christmas vacation. We dated again during spring vacation and then when I got home from school.

"Back at the university in the fall, I got into an argument with the athletic director's aide about the financial aid, that wasn't the way it was supposed to be. I was supposed to be able to live in a house again and have a job to pay for my meals and room and board. He said that they would fix that up. I stayed on for a weekend, but I just didn't have the money to keep going. I didn't have a job, and I hadn't gotten a place to live. And, frankly, didn't have enough clothes to do me much good. And I thought 'the hell with it. If they want me to play football, they are going to have to do better than this. If they don't I'm going home.' So I went to see the chief coach, Eddy Anderson, and told him that I was going home, and if they wanted me back they were going to have to change things. I never heard from them again, and I didn't have to go back. That was the end of my college career.

"Over the summer period my drinking was about the same. I drank, I suppose, every Saturday night. I usually went out on a little spree with three or four other people. I usually wound up drinking too much, but it never got out of control. I had a loss of memory in high school when I got drunk two or three times. Loss of memory has been something that plagued me all the time I drank.

"Summer came to an end, and I went to work on a construction job. I worked that fall of 1942 on a construction crew with the telephone company. My drinking was on weekends or rainy days. One thing that you have to understand is that when you're working on construction gangs, rainy days and days off of work are hard drinking days. Everyone drinks hard. That's what I grew up with; it's what I lived with. We were a hard drinking bunch of young men and old men, whatever you want to call them.

"In December I had my second round of pneumonia and almost died. I was laid up for three and a half or four weeks. That was before penicillin. They didn't have the rapid antibiotic recovery rate that you have now. You toughed it out with sulfa and whatever other stuff they had available. It was a bad experience. I had pneumonia two or three times."[2]

Notes

1 From recordings made by Harold Hughes in anticipation of his writing a book.
2 Ibid.

As a soldier in the army in World War II, Harold Hughes fought in Sicily, Italy, and North Africa, won several decorations, and was court-martialed for assaulting an officer. Photo: Personal family photo used with permission of the Hughes family.

Hughes with wife, Eva, and their young family (from left) Connie and Carol. Carol was born while he was away at war and this photo was taken not long after he returned, and met her for the first time. Photo: Personal family photo used with permission of the Hughes family.

CHAPTER FIVE

Jesse's Death and Harold's Military Service

"In Africa, we were located in a town and were supposed to hold the town for three days. I was lying on a pile of ammunition boxes. All I remember is white fire and blue flames, smoke, and my head ringing like hell. I rolled over on the ground and looked right into the top of the head of a friend of mine whose head had been blown off right above his eyes. It suddenly happened that my heart was strangely warmed." [1]

HAROLD E. HUGHES

Hughes and Jesse, his older brother, were very close. They grew up going to school together. They played sports together and hunted, fished, and trapped together. They tended to the garden and later worked at many odd jobs to help their family survive. Then one night Jesse was killed in an automobile accident and Harold's life was changed drastically.

Phyllis Hughes Ewing recalled the tragedy: "This was six months after Pearl Harbor. Jesse had been drafted into the Army and was about to leave on the bus to go to basic training. He and his best friend were taking their girlfriends out one last time. They went to a dance in Storm Lake, Iowa. On the drive home from the dance late at night, there was a violent storm. They hit a bridge abutment somewhere between Storm Lake and Ida Grove. The creek was swollen with rainwater. The car flipped over into the creek and all four of the kids were killed — my Uncle Jesse, his best friend, and both of the girls. It was a terrible blow to the community — all four of these young people dying at once.

"My grandmother never recovered because everybody said that Jesse was the one that took after her. He had her red hair from the Irish side, blue eyes from his dad. My dad sort of took after the darker

Indian side I think. Jesse's death had a devastating effect on Dad's life. A couple of times when we were driving back and forth, my dad would say, 'that's the bridge where your Uncle Jesse died.'

"A few months prior to Jesse's death, my dad started dating Minerva, my mother's sister. After a while, they broke up, and Dad started dating my mother, Eva. They got married and soon after, Dad was drafted into the Army.[2]

Regarding drinking in the Army, Hughes reported: "I didn't drink at all for about two months. Frankly, I didn't have any money. I sent all of my money home to Eva. We had one baby and just before I left, Eva became pregnant. We were hoping to see each other again before I shipped out, but when we finished our basic training, they split up my unit. I could have gone to OCS, Officers Candidate School, but I turned it down, frankly, because I was inspired with the thought that I wanted to go and fight. That's the way I felt. I didn't want to fool around and be a ninety-day wonder. I just wanted to get the hell out and go with the men. They split off a half dozen or so of us and sent us over to Georgia. The 83rd Chemical Battalion was just preparing to ship out to Africa. So by the time I got there and got equipped, I'd been trained in chemical warfare service. At that point we didn't know whether we were going to be using chemical warfare or gas or what.

"In Africa, we were located in a town and were supposed to hold the town for three days. I was lying on a pile of ammunition boxes. All I remember is white fire and blue flames, smoke, and my head ringing like hell. I rolled over on the ground and looked right into the top of the head of a friend of mine whose head had been blown off right above his eyes. I started vomiting. I reacted, just reacted like mad. I turned over the other way, and there laid a limey with a piece of steel sticking out through his chest and screaming, 'My God help me breathe!' Blood was gurgling out of his mouth. Well, to make a long story short, we took quite a bit of damage.

"Then I was sent out to an outpost that night up on the mountain. That was one of the awfulest nights I ever spent. I was scared to death. My friends were dead, some dying. It had a hell of an effect on me, that particular incident did. It was just out of the blue. Suddenly you're out there alone. The commandos had lost two men in a neighboring outpost the night before. A German patrol came in and cut their throats. Of course when you're out there alone, you and one other guy, it's a pretty awful experience. We've had a lot of men do that for a lot of years, so you're no different than anyone else. But after the loss of men, heavy fire, and one thing and another, and the loss of my ammunition carrier, I gave up hope for living at that point."[3]

Hughes continues, "I never thought I'd get home again. It suddenly dawned on me that the odds are ten to one of getting killed in any single engagement, and about, I suppose, ten to one that you wouldn't be killed. About one out of ten would get killed. About three out of ten would be wounded. And about five wouldn't. But the odds were running out. We were losing a lot of men. We were there at that period of time when all hell broke out.

"I had contracted malaria, but I didn't realize it. I was getting sicker and sicker every day; but I didn't say anything about it. But we went up into the mountains into a pass where the American troops broke out of the beachhead. We moved out from the commandos and joined the American troops. We hadn't slept for the last three days. We were taking pills to stay awake. I don't know what they were.

"We were trying to hold down the road and the highway, which we did. But when we moved up into the mountains, the last thing I remember was wandering around up the road. Then a medic stopped me and asked me what the hell was wrong. I said, 'By God, I don't know. But I'm burning up and sicker than hell, and I just haven't got the strength to walk another step.' He stuck a thermometer in my mouth, got me to lie down and said, 'My God you have a temperature of 106.6.' I will never forget that. 'We've got to get you out of here right now.' So they put me on some sort of vehicle that was going back down to a beach. I laid on the beach for about a day.

"No one ever bothered to tell me that with jaundice you are subject to depression. No one ever bothered telling me that with jaundice you shouldn't have a drink. I was born with jaundice. Hell, I didn't know you suffered depression from jaundice and that you shouldn't drink when you have bad jaundice because your liver doesn't have the capacity to handle the liquor. It does injury and damage to it. Anyway, I recovered.

"They sent me to a combat reconditioning battalion outside of Auron, and I spent thirty days in there combat reconditioning, drinking, fighting, you name it. That's where I got court martialed. I was in Auron one night on leave. We got in an argument in a theatre with some officers over something or another. I don't remember what it was. It doesn't matter anyway. Two or three of us had missed the last transportation to camp anyway. We were of course AWOL (Absent With Out Leave), not intentionally. We just missed the damn truck that took us back. So we got in a fistfight and wound up in the stockade. The first thing I remember was waking up and looking at those damned floodlights behind a barbed-wire barricade wondering what the hell happened. I really had no clear memory of it."[4]

Hughes recalls, "The next morning they drug us through court-martial proceedings. They fined me two-thirds of my pay and sentenced me to six months in the stockade but suspended the sentence to send me back to my combat unit. I'll never forget the major that was there said, 'You're probably going to get killed anyway, so that's the best way to handle it.' That was a nice send-off to a guy who's sick and miserable and sorry and hates himself anyway. He hasn't had any mail for six months. He doesn't much give a damn at that point whether he lives or dies or anything else. That's where I was.

"Back to the reconditioning battalion. When we finished that, they put us on an old liberty ship and sent us back to Italy. It took us fifteen days to cross the Mediterranean. We were under sub attack three or four times in the crossing. It was in the winter and the weather was bad. It was rough. It was a very bad crossing. We finally landed at Naples. They signed me back to my old company, my old outfit again. I went back with them. In the meantime, on January 26 they had made the invasion of Anzio. I wasn't with my unit. My company had been on an LCI (Landing Craft Infantry) that ran into a minefield and sank. Two-thirds of my company died when that thing went down. The survivors were sent back to Naples to a staging area for replacements and I joined them about the middle of replacements.

"Then we went up to the Southern front. It was the Black Cat Division — British troops spying by Monte Casino with another British division. Intermittently the drinking went on in those periods whenever I could get booze. Everyone else was drinking too. I didn't think I was any different than anyone else. I wasn't screwing around. I was just drinking. I can honestly say that as far as playing the [prostitutes] and everything that was going on commonly, right and left and upside-down, I wasn't involved in that. I was involved in the drinking, raising hell, and fighting. You know when you get a bunch of guys drinking, it isn't long before they get into a fight.

"So we came back from there. Then we went back to the Anzio beachhead after a couple of weeks. Then back to Magnolia. Then from the beachhead, I left and went back to the racetrack. From there, back to the states. This was July 10, 1945."[5]

The effects of war would stay with him for some time. Phyllis recalls that when Hughes returned from the service he experienced what is now understood as PTSD (Post-Traumatic Stress Disorder). She recalls several times that when a loud sound would occur in the neighborhood or fireworks near the Fourth of July, he would bound out of bed and take a stance on his knees as if he were shouldering his Browning automatic rifle. After a moment or two, he would wake up, Eva would console him, and he would return to bed.

In spite of his drinking and his horrific experience in the war, Hughes was beginning to exhibit some of the qualities that would help him launch his political career.

Notes

1 From recordings made by Harold Hughes in anticipation of his writing a book.
2 Phyllis Hughes Ewing, Hughes' youngest daughter
3 From recordings made by Harold Hughes in anticipation of his writing a book.
4 Ibid.
5 Ibid.

The Governor's wife, Mrs. Harold E. Hughes, in her role as First Lady of Iowa.
Photo: Johnson Photographers, Clinton, Iowa, State Historical Society of Iowa, Des Moines.

CHAPTER SIX

Eva Hughes, an Angel

"My mother had a lot of challenges in her life with what today would have been called mental illness. Back then, mental illness was not understood; it was a deep, dark secret to be covered up." [1]

PHYLLIS HUGHES EWING

No story about Senator Hughes is complete without discussing the role that his first wife, Eva, played in his life. Hughes and Eva were married in Ida Grove, Iowa on August 11, 1941. They had three daughters — Connie, Carol, and Phyllis. Harold once referred to Eva as "an angel sent to him by God."

In about mid-1940, Eva Mercer and her family moved from Holstein, Iowa to Ida Grove. Eva was in high school. Harold Hughes was home from the University of Iowa for the summer and was a lifeguard at the local pool. Eva liked to swim and spent a lot of time at the pool. Harold didn't waste any time. He swept Eva off her feet.

The two were married in August of 1941. They lived together in Ida Grove for the next fifteen years and raised their three daughters. Their marriage was turbulent, especially in the early years when Hughes was drinking. On several occasions, Eva left him and went to live with her mother for brief periods of time. On one occasion she attempted to have him committed to a state mental hospital because of his drinking. However, during this time Hughes quit drinking. After fifteen years, they moved to Des Moines where they remained together through Harold's six years as governor and six years as U.S. senator.

A *Washington Post* article describes Eva: "Eva Hughes is a dark-haired, pretty, warm woman who seems to have conquered the bouts of shyness she had as a governor's wife." The other day she bustled around the house, wrapping Christmas presents, among them, photo albums. They contained pictures taken over the years of herself, Hughes, and the only one of three daughters unmarried: Phyllis, who just graduated from high school last year. Also prominent in the pictures was their Irish setter who is so fiercely loyal to Mrs. Hughes that when the senator kisses his wife good-bye, he has to put the dog on the sun deck for fear the dog will attack. 'He seems to just go after men,' Mrs. Hughes said."

The article continues, "Reading is their (the Hughes') number one hobby. Both lean toward philosophy, religion, mysticism, and metaphysics. Asked if he believed in ESP and psychic powers, the Senator said, 'Sure do.'

"Mrs. Hughes catalogues books by subject and authors — and some other books spill over in piles on the floor …

"Mrs. Hughes says she and her husband 'come to the parting of the ways' on television. She watches news and some sports programs; he watches late movies — 'especially if it's a good western, like High Noon. Their musical tastes lean toward hymns and she says 'I'm a Les Elgart fan.'"[2]

"Mrs. Hughes enjoys music and is one accomplished musician. While in high school she played clarinet in the Ida Grove band, going with the band to the national contest in Minneapolis, Minnesota. The next year it was held in Iowa City, and the third year in Kansas City, Missouri. She also plays piano."[3]

While Hughes was governor, the couple joined Spiritual Frontiers Fellowship and the Society for Psychical Research, a British organization committed to spiritualism and psychic phenomena. Phyllis has indicated that Gene Kieffer, publicity and marketing professional and friend of Hughes, introduced Harold and Eva to that arena of interest.

When Hughes was governor, Eva became deeply involved in spiritualism and related subjects. She read books about the well-known spiritualist medium, Arthur Ford. Eva remained interested in psychic phenomena throughout her life, exchanging letters with friends who shared her interest.

Their daughter, Phyllis, recalled that her mother "had years when she was quite normal and loveable." She also recalled that her dad and mother and the girls had many years of good times together. My mother was a good mother except when she had episodes of mental illness."

Phyllis reluctantly gave a candid and little known side of her mother. She recalled, "My mother grew up in Holstein, Iowa. Her father was a newspaperman before he died. His untimely death left my grandmother with four children. Their life was very difficult. My father once said that his family was 'poor but nothing like Eva's family.' In those days there was no social welfare, no social security. Life was very difficult for them.

"My mother had a lot of challenges in her life that today would be called mental illness. Back then mental illness was not understood; it was a deep, dark secret to be covered up. That was especially true if you were in political public life. You had to keep it covered up. I think there were other factors with my mother. She had a huge, what they called a nervous breakdown, a year before I was born. She was in a mental institution in either Omaha or Kansas City. At one point, they were about to give her shock treatments, but she did not want them. She begged my father to bring her home and not let them give her shock treatments. He tried to get her released but the institution would not release her. He literally picked her up, carried her out of the hospital in a gown, and brought her home to Ida Grove the night before they were going to begin shock treatments. At that point she was in one of her terrible spirals.

"She had some sort of a major, mental event about once a decade. From what I've read, I think it might have been some type of bipolar condition. When I read about the bipolar condition, I said, 'Whoa, that is my mother.' She just leapt off the page. She was also a lifelong bulimic. She would have years that were bad. She would have herself all whipped up in a frenzy. She would believe in conspiracies, crazy things, and we would have to try to keep her calm.

"As soon as I came home from school, I would stay with her and keep her calm so she wouldn't do anything crazy. When she had the episode the year before I was born, my father said that she was not in the best mental shape when she was pregnant with me. He wasn't sure she'd be able to care for me as an infant. He thought he might have to have my grandmother take care of me. When I was born, she snapped out of it and was more like her normal self.

"Big changes would set her off and send her into one of those spirals. She had a terrible year the first year Dad was governor. She had another terrible year the first year he was senator. These transitions, these big changes in her life, had a way of setting her off."[4]

Elaine Estes, past director of the Des Moines Public Library, remembers when she and Hughes' Aunt Esther, who also worked at the library, helped groom Eva for the challenges of being the First Lady of Iowa. They helped her with wardrobe and social etiquette. They introduced her to professional women's organization where she could build new relationships. Estes remembers Eva as a very beautiful and humble person and that she gracefully rose to the occasion of the social responsibilities of her new position as the First Lady of Iowa.

Since Hughes enjoyed fishing and hunting, there were always several guns in the house. Phyllis recalls an occasion when her mother was in one of her manic episodes that her dad advised her: "If you ever hear a gunshot from the house, don't go in. Just call the police. I'm concerned that in one of her episodes, she might shoot me."

Phyllis continues, "After years of struggling, mother finally wound up in Iowa City with a wonderful doctor. He put her on some psychiatric meds that she'd not been on before, some anti-depressants. It really just snapped her out of it. She calmed down after a few weeks. When she came out of Iowa City that year, she and my father were in the process of what would be a very bitter divorce. She was really changed. She overcame that attention deficit thing where she was always jittery, shifting from one thing to another. She was calm when you'd have a conversation with her. She'd look you in the eye steadily and finish a sentence without jumping to something else. She seemed to have let go of all her crazy theories about this and that. I thought, 'Wow, the pill she's on, let's be sure to keep that coming.'

One little pill and all of a sudden, she could be normal again. That was a first for me. She quit taking them after a few months. They made her mouth dry and upset her sleep cycle."[5]

The Hughes had been married for 45 years when Harold filed for divorce in 1987. According to Phyllis, they had many good years. There were tense times when Eva had her manic episodes, but all in all, Phyllis considers the marriage to have been quite compatible. Perhaps Eva's mental illness contributed to the divorce. We are not likely to ever know.

After a long and bitter divorce, Harold and Eva parted. Eva returned to Des Moines where she lived until she died on January 25, 2017. Harold married a second time, to Julianne Holm.

Notes

1 Phyllis Hughes Ewing, Harold Hughes' youngest daughter
2 MacPherson, Myra, "The Rise and Rise of Harold Hughes," *The Washington Post*, Sunday December 20, 1970, Washington, D.C.
3 Wadsworth, Margaret, "What's Cooking in Nevada," *Nevada Journal*, the Nevada, Colo, and Collins newspaper.
4 Phyllis Hughes Ewing, Harold Hughes' youngest daughter
5 Ibid.

Harold and Eva Hughes at the 1959 Inaugural Ball for Governor Herschel Loveless, Iowa's 34th governor. Eva had a wonderful sense of style which was served her well as she transitioned into her role as Iowa's First Lady in 1962. Photo: Courtesy Conley Wolterman, historic archives, Ida Grove, Iowa.

Harold and Eva Hughes on a leisurely tandem bicycle ride.
Photo: State Historical Society of Iowa, Des Moines.

Eva Hughes and June Wilson (the author's wife) were lifelong friends, shown here at the Wilson's fiftieth anniversary celebration in 1999.
Photo: Personal photo used with permission of June Wilson.

Harold Godberson (left), and Reverend Clifford Isaacson, visit with Harold Hughes during fellowship hour following church service at the United Methodist Church in Ida Grove, Iowa in the 1960s. Photo: Courtesy Conley Wolterman, historic archives, Ida Grove, Iowa.

CHAPTER SEVEN

Hughes' Christian Faith

"I pray over the decisions that I have made.
I have felt that my reason in being in public life was
to be of service to my fellow man.
To me there is a relationship between my political life
and my Christian heritage and belief." [1]

HAROLD E. HUGHES

"Religion, for many, little more than a perfunctory exercise in church-going, has been of major importance to Harold E. Hughes — "the motivating force in my life' he has said.

"Religion played a central part in Hughes' career as a U.S. senator, and before that, as Iowa governor. He says, in fact, 'I think God led me into public service,' and he prayed before making each decision on whether to continue in public life."[2]

According to Hughes, "From the earliest days of my life, my family was a very religious family. We went to church on Sundays, always to the Methodist church in Iowa. Although my mother and father had been Baptists in Kentucky, there was no Baptist Church in Ida Grove. I suppose that was as close to their denominational beliefs as they could come. As a result, they had their letters transferred to the Methodist church. So I was born and baptized into the Methodist church. I have been a member of that same little Methodist church in Ida Grove, Iowa, all the days of my life.

"My wife grew up in a Methodist church in Holstein, Iowa. We both participated in the same youth activities between the two churches of Holstein and Ida Grove. We went to church and Sunday school every Sunday morning.

"I remember one time finding a dime in one of the pews after church and begging to stop at the newsstand to buy some candy. But my mother said I had to put it in the collection plate the next Sunday, that it wasn't right to keep it. I had difficulty understanding that. As a matter of fact, I still do. Anyway, that was my heritage.

"I remember that all those years my grandfather and grandmother both taught Sunday school classes. We prayed every time we went to their house. Grace was said at every meal. My grandfather used to teach me to pray at his knee. We had a deeply religious concept, and background, and faith in God.

"The night after I graduated from high school, I left home to go to the University of Iowa. I went there to work on the campus for the summer to pay for my tuition and books. The only reason I bring it up is that when I was at the University of Iowa, I didn't continue going to church or Sunday school. I didn't participate in any religious activities. As a matter of fact, from that point until about 1946 or 1947, I didn't go back to church. However, after my discharge from the Army and getting back with my family, we did start going to church.

"When I quit drinking, I decided to turn my life over to God as I understood Him. Many things in my religious experience had troubled me. As a boy growing up, many times I had been lonely, distant, and spent a great deal of time thinking about spiritual values of life. I had a couple of relatives in Kentucky who had been ministers. I thought about entering the ministry. I felt a closeness to God, a kinship, a spiritual relationship, but I strayed from it during my drinking years and never came back to it until toward the close of those years.

"At that point, a minister came into Ida Grove who became a lifelong friend, Dr. Wayne Shoemaker. He encouraged my activity in the church as a churchman. He was a man I could talk to, a man I could question and get answers. If he didn't know the answers, we'd look for them together. He was understanding and tolerant. He got me interested in church work. I soon became a member of the official board and the finance commission. I sang in the choir and even sang for funerals and an occasional wedding.

"Wayne also asked me if I would teach a Sunday school class. The Sunday school class sent me to seeking. It was a high school Sunday school class that had declined to only five or six members because of lack of interest. In my discussions with Dr. Shoemaker, I told him that I would teach Sunday school if I could teach from the Bible and no other way. And the students really made a student out of me. I started pursuing the Scripture, studying, and I thought at that point some about entering the ministry. In fact, I talked to Dr. Shoemaker about it. He showed me the courses in the Methodist church I could follow. First, I could become a lay speaker, later on a lay preacher, and then perhaps finish up my college and seminary work and become an ordained minister.

"I took courses to become a licensed lay speaker in the Methodist church. In fact, I still have some of the dissertations that I wrote in preparation of that. On numerous occasions, I filled pulpits for vacationing ministers and those who were sick in some of the small churches around northwest Iowa. I remember the first time I was ever in a pulpit, however. It was in my own church of Ida Grove on laymen's Sunday when Dr. Shoemaker asked me to speak. It was a critical experience for me. I felt that many of the people in the congregation might view me as a sinner rather than someone who could speak of spiritual things.

"These were growing years for me, speaking, understanding, pursuing the Spirit, and things began to happen in my personal life. I began to believe really in the Scripture. I wanted answers to the questions, to seek them, to study them, to get Bible commentaries. Dr. Shoemaker helped me. Reverend Russell Wilson, who was then the minister of the Church of God in Ida Grove, also helped me. Along with another minister who was a Presbyterian, Reverend Carl Sinning, all three of these Protestant ministers became very good friends of mine. In my work in the field of alcoholism, they all helped me. They worked with members of their own congregations when we became fast and steady friends. And as a result of that, all the years of my life in one way or another, we have been working together on spiritual programs and social programs.

"I am indebted to the fact that God brought together such a group of men. They have been lasting friends to me all of these years. I value so highly their confidence and faith in me as a human being and their belief in God. They helped me in those years to find a lasting faith in a Supreme Being through Jesus Christ. I've never been ashamed of Him.

"Those years that I taught the high school class were the growing years of my life. They continued when I later went to Des Moines as a member of the Commerce Commission and went to the West Des Moines Methodist Church. They asked me to teach their high school class. I taught the class, as a matter of fact, for two years. Over the period of years that I taught that class, I had at least two members of my class who later became ordained ministers. A number of others have gone into spirituality-related work. I guess if a man is entitled to have some pride, the fact that perhaps I had some effect on the lives of those young people gives me pride. I may have helped them to have faith in God as I had been helped."[3]

In regard to making decisions, Hughes recorded: "Every time I have made a decision to run for public office, in the final analysis, it has been a private decision with my family and myself. I've thought about it. I prayed over the decisions that I have made. I have felt that my reason for being in public life was to be of service to my fellow man. To me there is a direct relationship between my political life and my Christian heritage and beliefs. I've said many times that politics has been my ministry — that I considered entering the church as a minister — but I eventually rejected that idea because I didn't feel that my personality was compatible with the organized church. But my desire has always been to try and make, wherever I am, a little better place to live.

"I know that sounds corny. Nonetheless it's the truth. Politics was a way to do that. I felt I had the ability to do it. A lot of people questioned my ability because they didn't have the opportunity to know me well enough. But I had confidence in my own ability.

"The reason I undertook the (political) race was that I thought there were things that desperately needed doing. Things were going undone. I had some ideas and my friends had some ideas that were worthy of fighting for. I felt there was a strong purpose in running even though victory wasn't assured. The running itself serves a good purpose. It helps to increase the public discussion, the debate, on the critical issues and the needs of our time. I felt the energy and the effort that I put forth was constructive. In the final analysis, I had to accept the fact that we were running against odds that were overwhelming and the possibility of winning was quite remote. We lived with that reality constantly and that every step of the way was uphill. I had to do it. I've said a lot of times that something in me seems to drive me on. I feel a mission in life to do what I can wherever I am to try and alleviate suffering and pain. And to also broaden the knowledge and understanding of all of us. At times I have succeeded. At times I haven't, I guess. That was one of the basic reasons for running."[4]

Hughes continued: "One night during my third term as governor, I received a telephone call at about 11 pm after I'd been asleep for an hour. I'd been working hard with practically no sleep for weeks. The call was from a fellow AA member who was living in a nearby town. He had worked for me in one of my earlier terms but had quit. He said he hadn't worked for six months. He wanted me to give him a job right over the phone. He started crying and said he had to get his children presents for Christmas. I knew he was in need, but I didn't know how great his need was. I pleaded for him to go to bed and come in at ten o'clock in the morning. 'Okay,' he said dejectedly. The next morning his wife called me and told me he had killed himself.

"The episode shook me a great deal. Lots of thoughts go through your mind when something like this happens. I could have asked him to come to the mansion, I thought. I could have gotten dressed and driven the forty minutes to see him. I'd been doing things like that for years. But I didn't.

"I knew from that moment on that I could never refuse another person's call for help. I had a hard time not blaming myself for his death. But it was through experiences like this and with my daughter, Carol's death at the age of thirty-two, that I began to understand and accept God's forgiveness.

"Shortly after we moved to Washington, Carol got involved in the Jesus Movement. Eva and I observed a joy and happiness in her life we'd never seen before. Many an evening was spent with the family talking together about Jesus Christ.

"It was because of Carol's new faith that I initially began to ask myself if I had ever committed my life to Jesus Christ. Even in politics, church work, or serving my fellow man, I certainly had not found the forgiveness and self-acceptance she had found.

"Accepting God's, or as far as that's concerned, any person's help, has always been a problem for me. Probably because I've always seen myself as a strong, independent person and didn't need anyone's help.

"But in the last three years since we've been in Washington, D.C., two other people came into my life who had a profound effect on me. I had been attending the Senate Prayer Breakfast, which met each week in the Capitol, and I noticed that two men who always attended, Doug Coe and Dick Halverson, never spoke. I later found out that they were leaders behind the prayer breakfast work.

"Doug and Dick became brothers to me in much the way that Wayne Shoemaker and Father Dailey had been in Ida Grove. Doug was persistent. After every Wednesday prayer breakfast, he came by my office. He was the first person, while I was in office, who ever asked me to pray. I'd asked people before, but no one had asked me. Dick became my spiritual teacher and had much to do with my coming to understand Christ's love and acceptance.

Though Hughes was proud of many of his political accomplishments, in the end, his commitment to God and to his faith, and his desire to devote time to ministering to man's spiritual needs determined his decision in 1972 to leave the Senate. "Some good people have said that my decision to leave public service at this time is a 'cop-out.' I can understand how they could interpret it that way with the pressures a man in public life now faces and with the majority of the American public now thinking that all politicians are corrupt. I recently had a young man in my office who asked if I thought I was being a 'responsible leader' by leaving the Senate. He implied he thought I wasn't. I told him I felt I was more responsible because I believe I can best change the political base of this land by working from a spiritual base. Because I believe you can't change people politically until they've changed spiritually. If I did not follow the dictates of my conscience and my God, I would be less responsible.

"I'm not sure which direction God will lead me, but after January 1, 1975, I plan to take a period for prayer, study, and meditation, and then get back into the arena of people's problems. I do not have long on this earth. The rest of my time I want my total energies given to helping young people, drug addicts, alcoholics, and couples whose marriages are cracking up."

Later, Hughes recorded, "I've been able to help a few colleagues in government and their wives who've had difficulties with alcohol and other problems. I want to keep working with government leaders, encouraging them in building their relationships with God and their fellow man. I want to serve our President and our people. I believe my decision to leave the Senate, rather than being a cop-out, will provide a new platform for me to tackle the troubles our leaders and people face.

"Abraham Lincoln, on nine different occasions, asked that the nation set a day for prayer, fasting, and repentance. I believe our nation is in no less need of prayer today. So at this time when our nation faces a crisis of the Spirit, I want my new life devoted to mobilizing people to see God with all their hearts.

"The writer of Chronicles [in the Bible] expresses what I see as our paramount concern: 'If my people who are called by my name humble themselves and pray and seek my face, and turn from their wicked ways, then I will hear from heaven, and will forgive their sin and heal their land.'[3]

"I believe this portion of Scripture points to the important need now. I think this is more important than my serving in the Senate or even the White House. I want to humble myself, pray, seek His face, and turn from my wicked ways. I hope others do too. Maybe in this way we can see the healing of our land."[4]

In addition to his Christian beliefs in the Holy Trinity and the power of prayer, Hughes also believed that when people die they continue to exist in a "spiritual state." He said that he communicated with his deceased brother, Jesse, through a spiritual medium. Hughes believed that some people are able to see the future, as did the prophets of the Old Testament. The Senator believed some people have the gift of being able to heal other people. He and his family occasionally attended a church in Washington, D.C., where healing was a part of the service.

Hughes also believed that some people possess extrasensory perception. That is, they can communicate with others through thoughts alone. He and Eva were interested in psychic phenomena and the occult. He himself had a psychic gift of perceiving the lives of some deceased individuals.

The following story describes Hughes' response to evangelist Kathryn Kuhlman's touch during a healing service and illustrates an experience that moved him.

The Senator Floats Away

The Washingtonian reported that "Hughes was speaking at the Delamarva Evangelistic Church on Thursday night in April of 1979. About a thousand people attended the service at the church on the edge of Salisbury, thirty miles inland from Ocean City on Maryland's Eastern Shore.

"It was an evangelistic service filled with the curious and the charismatics, those near belief, those wanting it, and those transported on its other side — and by large joyful events, animated by the presence of a nice and certain God, powered by the need to spread His Holy Word. And because he believes, deeply, Harold Hughes can go with the flow."[5]

"I stood in the pulpit at one of Kathryn Kuhlman's services," Hughes tells the congregation, referring to the faith healer. "She touched me, and I want to tell you, I floated right away into heaven. I fell ten feet out of that pulpit, hit the floor, and didn't feel a thing. When I woke up, I was looking at the bottom of the piano. The whole audience, four thousand of them, were standing up and cheering and hollering, and I didn't think I had made an ass of myself at all. I never felt so good. For twenty-four hours I was floating. I know these things happen."[6]

Notes

1 Kotz, Nick and Risser, James, "Messiah from the Midwest?," *The Washington Monthly*, May 1970.
2 Ibid.
3 II Chronicles 7:14, *The Holy Bible*, Revised Standard Version, published 1952, Harper and Brothers, New York
4 From recordings made by Harold Hughes in anticipation of his writing a book.
5 Means, Howard, *The Prophet, The Washingtonian*, Washington, D.C., July 1979
6 Ibid.
7 Brod, Ruth Hagy, *Ena Twigg: Medium*, W. H. Allen London, 1975, pp. 181-183

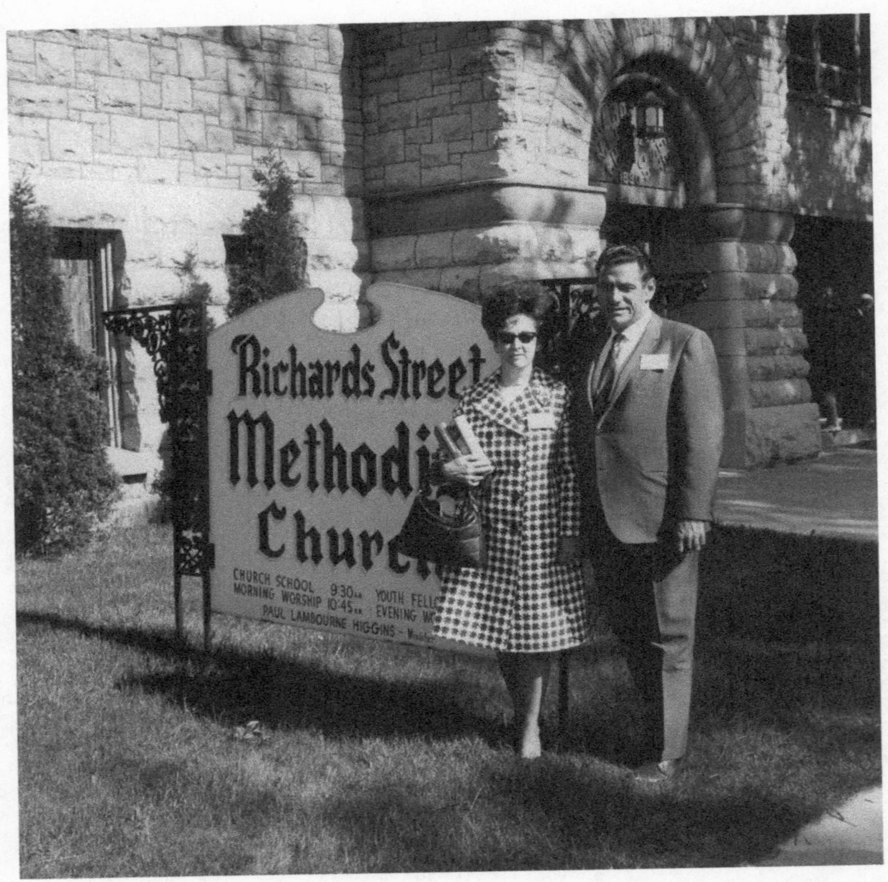

Harold Hughes and his wife, Eva, in Joliet, Illinois, attending a Spiritual Frontiers Fellowship gathering in 1969. Photo: Personal photo used with permission of the Hughes family.

CHAPTER EIGHT

Hughes and the Paranormal

"During a conference, Arthur Ford, one of the most well known spiritualist mediums of that era, invited Hughes and me to attend a séance with a dozen to fifteen other people. During the séance, a voice communicated with me through Ford acknowledging my part in the creation of the Iowa Comprehensive Alcoholism Project and wishing me success. Hughes later told me that he knew the man who spoke through Ford when he was alive and that he was involved in work with alcoholics."

RUSSELL L. WILSON

Phyllis Hughes Ewing recalls her dad's involvement in spiritualism and psychic phenomena.

"My dad had a friend named Gene Kieffer. He came into my parents' orbit and handled advertising and media stuff for various campaigns. Gene was into that stuff (spiritualism and the paranormal) and introduced it to my parents. To be fair, my dad was sort of into it but my mother really got into it and didn't want to let it go.

"My dad wanted to stay more in the Christian mainstream. My mom and dad basically stayed within their Christian roots."

According to Phyllis, her mother's, and perhaps to a lesser degree, her father's interest in spiritualism and survival after death, were related to her sister, Carol's, life-long struggle with illnesses. Perhaps the Hughes' interest in survival after death was the result of knowing that Carol would not live long. "My mother and Carol were very close, and my mother needed some concrete proof that people who die are still with us," said Phyllis. Carol died at the young age of thirty-two.

On a spring day in 1967 the governor's top aide, Dwight Jensen, called Russ Wilson, who now served on the Board of Control of the State of Iowa for Governor Hughes, and told him the governor wanted him to go on a trip with him leaving the next day. It was not an official state trip and he would be responsible for his meals and any other expenses.

Early the next morning, Hughes and Wilson boarded a private D-18 Beech piloted by Colonel Milford Juhl and D.C. Powell. They headed for Chicago where they attended a Spiritual Frontiers Fellowship meeting, a large gathering of faith healers, psychics, spiritual mediums, advocates of the paranormal and their followers.

Among the speakers was a Catholic priest from England who described several exorcisms of demonic spirits. Faith healers discussed what they described as "miraculous" healings. Arthur Ford, one of the most well-known spiritualist mediums of that era, invited Hughes and Wilson to attend a séance he was holding during the conference.

The séance was attended by a dozen to fifteen people. During the séance a voice communicated with Wilson through Ford acknowledging Wilson's part in the creation of the Iowa Comprehensive Alcoholism Project and wishing him success. Hughes later told Wilson that he knew the man who spoke through Ford when he was alive and that he was involved in work with alcoholics.

Another voice came through the medium and communicated with Hughes, but Wilson cannot recall the content. However, he does recall while at the conference attending a private session with Irene Hughes (no relation), a well-known psychic who wrote a regular column on psychic phenomena and spiritualism in a prominent newspaper in the Chicago area. Irene predicted that Hughes would run for the U.S. Senate and be successful. In that session the alleged voice of Henry A. Wallace, former Vice President of the United States and former resident of Des Moines, communicated with him. Wallace instructed him to communicate with his son, Henry B. Wallace, who was then living on Ashworth Road in West Des Moines. Wallace told Hughes to tell his son his plan to run for the Senate, and to tell him he should support Hughes financially. Whether or not Hughes contacted Henry B., we'll never know. Harold and Irene Hughes became friends and communicated by letter and phone several times after that meeting.

After attending the conference, Hughes and Wilson boarded the D-18 Beech and flew to Indianapolis where the governor was the featured speaker at the Jefferson-Jackson Dinner in Indianapolis. Hughes gave a rousing speech and was warmly received.

During the speech, Colonel Juhl had been monitoring the weather and was aware that two strong thunderstorms were converging between Indianapolis and Des Moines. They needed to leave immediately. The mayor of Indianapolis arranged for a police escort to the airport. Col. Juhl had the engines warmed up. In a few minutes they were on their way.

British author Ruth Hagy Brod further illustrates Hughes' interest in psychic powers in her writing about British spiritualist and medium Ena Twigg,: "Each month seemed to bring new surprises. In September we were visited by three senators who came to the house for sittings. Two wished to remain incognito. The third was Senator Harold Hughes, accompanied by his wife. The senator bravely and openly declared his belief in survival and told the press that he had sat with mediums and communicated with his dead brother. He and his wife signed my guest book. The senator is a member of the Spiritual Frontiers Fellowship and belongs to our British Society for Psychical Research. He has spoken in the Reverend William Rauscher's church and for other SFF churches and groups. That this man, who is deeply spiritual and a natural psychic, should find these qualities handicaps, instead of assets in aspiring towards the presidency, is a sad commentary of our times. After all, Abraham Lincoln had a medium sit with him in the White House, and George Washington saw visions — and they were both great American presidents.[1]

"Reverend Robert Lewis tells this wonderful story about Senator Hughes' psychic power: 'We had Senator Hughes and one of his aides to dinner at Bill Rauscher's prior to his speaking to our South Jersey Chapter of the Spiritual Frontiers Fellowship. After dinner was over, I handed him a picture of my grandmother, a picture that had allegedly cried real water tears my senior year in seminary when

I passed my examination. My grandmother had raised me, and we were very close.

"When Senator Hughes picked this picture up and held it, he said, 'This woman had an awful fall — from a second story.' This was true: She had fallen down a whole flight of stairs from the second story. The Senator said, 'She was a woman who he thought had had great faith and a wonderful soul.' This was all true. My grandmother was a Welsh Baptist and a very religious, prayerful woman, and she had tremendous influence on my background. The Welsh are very psychic, and my grandmother and her sister were psychic too. I am sure that is why I wanted to enter the ministry and have been so interested in the mystical.

"Then the senator described my little wagon and he saw me picking up something black — like coal — and putting it in a box. This was also true. Well, that was as vivid as a day in the life of my childhood. I had to pick coal because we were very poor, and my wagon was a homemade affair, with a box top. He told me other things about our family and myself — all of which were true. It was a very spontaneous thing and I would say the senator has great psychic powers."[2]

Russ Wilson recalls meeting with then Governor Hughes one morning, the day after one of the National Guard fighter jets stationed in Des Moines had crashed and killed the pilot. There was no apparent reason for the crash.

Hughes told Wilson that he had contacted the well-known psychic, Jean Dixon, regarding the crash and she described in detail the mechanical system that failed rendering the plane unmanageable resulting in the tragic crash.

Hughes' interest in the paranormal and parapsychology was no secret. He and Eva read a number of books by medium Arthur Ford, psychic healer Edgar Cayce, and others. In an article in the *Des Moines Register*, James Risser and George Anthon discussed Hughes' interest in psychic phenomena. "What he [Hughes] calls 'my search' led him to begin explaining the 'frontiers of the spirit' through belief and practices of such phenomena as extra perception, faith healing, and spiritualism.

"As a young man, Hughes goes off to fight in North Africa and Italy, and the horrors he saw as a combat soldier raised questions about the meaning of life that he found he could not answer.

"A factor, too, was the shock of his brother's death in an automobile accident — killed at twenty-three, squashed like a fly, for no apparent reason. Those personal crises, and the struggle to conquer alcoholism, launched Hughes on a consuming religious quest of a kind undertaken by few. 'I had to look for a purpose for being,' Hughes recalls. 'I had to find out why the immeasurable decision of this planet led men to destruction instead of creation.'

"He and his family have pursued psychic aspects of religion not as 'a sideshow' or as something 'bizarre,' the Iowa Democrat explains, "but as part of their attempt to better understand the relationship between man and his God, between man and the universe, to better perceive the meaning of their religion."[3]

Hughes once affirmed that, "I am a Christian and I am a Methodist." He also stated that he believed in "eternal life," that when people die physically, they continue to live spiritually.

Hughes affirmed his belief that some people have the ability to see the future.

Hughes and his family occasionally attended a Methodist church in Washington that practiced healing as part of the service.

The senator believed that certain mediums could establish communication with the spirit of the deceased. As mentioned, the governor attended a séance in Chicago with the well-known medium, Arthur Ford and he believed that he communicated with his deceased brother, Jesse Hughes through a medium. About a month before Hughes was sworn in as U.S. senator, he had a remarkable spiritual experience.

Notes

1 Brod, Ruth Hagy, *Ena Twigg: Medium*, W. H. Allen London, 1975, pp. 181-183

2 Ibid.

3 Risser, James and Anthon, George, "The Personal Religion of Harold E. Hughes," *Des Moines Register*, December 1971.

Harold Hughes with Arthur Ford, American psychic and founder of the Spiritual Frontiers Fellowship, circa 1967. Hughes would later believe that Mr. Ford was not entirely authentic, and distanced himself.
Photo: Personal photo used with permission of the Hughes family.

CHAPTER NINE

A Visit by "Two Men in White"

Just before I called you [Gene Kieffer] Friday morning, I was visited by 'two men in white' who stood just behind the sofa where you are sitting. They were eight feet tall. I know that because I took note of where their shoulders reached on the wall behind them, and after they left, I got a yardstick and measured the spot. They were eight feet tall.[1]

HAROLD E. HUGHES

In January of 1969 Gene Kieffer was in New York on business. Gene had been a political strategist and marketing advisor for Hughes' campaigns. Gene was very interested in psychic phenomena, clairvoyance, and faith healing. Phyllis Hughes believes he was responsible for introducing Hughes and Eva to those subjects.

In New York, on the way to the airport, Kieffer made an unannounced visit to a teacher of agnosticism, François Nesbitt. Among other things they discussed, Mr. Nesbitt told Kieffer about two books that, in his words, "would change the world." Kieffer was eager to purchase them. Serendipitously, Nesbitt knew that copies had arrived at a local bookstore the day before.

Kieffer went to Samuel Weiser's bookstore and purchased the books, *A Book of the Beginnings, Volumes I and II* by Gerald Massey. That morning, Governor Hughes called Kieffer and asked him to come to the governor's mansion when he got back to Des Moines. The governor had something to share with Gene.

Governor Hughes shared his experience of the "two men in white" with Russ Wilson in the governor's office the morning that it happened. Gene Kieffer's account, however, is much more detailed and is connected to the two mysterious books.

Kieffer recounts his arrival in Des Moines the next day. "When I went to the back door of the mansion, the governor was already there waiting for me. I began to tell him about the two books I was carrying, but he immediately stopped me. 'Don't say another word,' he said, holding up his hand, 'not until I tell you my story first. Come inside and follow me.' He led me up a flight of stairs to his study and asked me to sit on the sofa across from his favorite reading chair.

"'You know I've had my dreams and visions,' he said as he sat down facing me, 'but what I'm about to tell you was not a dream or a vision.'

"I was waiting for him to tell me his story, with the two Massey books still in the paper sack under my arm.

"'Just before I called you Friday morning, I was visited by two men in white who stood just behind the sofa where you are sitting. They were eight feet tall. I know that because I took note of where their shoulders reached on the wall behind them, and after they left, I got a yardstick and measured the spot. They were eight feet tall.'

"I said nothing but waited for the governor to continue." 'They said, "Ascertain for yourself that you are not having a dream or a vision," which I did by pinching my wrists, slapping my face, and I even got out of my chair to walk around the room and take a look out of the window. It was just beginning to snow.'

"'They said,' "Within twenty-four hours, two books will be found in New York City that will change the history of the world."

"Jesus, what do you think I have here," I said, pointing to the two books wrapped up in the paper sack under my arm."

"He said, 'Yes, I know. May I see them please?'"

"I unwrapped the books and handed them to the governor. He examined them for a moment and then laid them on a small table next to this chair and said, 'May I keep them overnight?'

"Sure, I said.

'Let's go downstairs. Eva has coffee and Christmas cookies for us.'

"So that's what we did. But no sooner had I taken a chair, when the governor excused himself. 'Oh, I just remembered,' he said. 'I have to make an important phone call. You and Eva can have your coffee and chat.'

"The next morning I stopped by the mansion to pick up the two books. The governor was on the back porch with them in hand and he passed them down to me as I sat in my car reaching up.

"What do you think?" I asked.

'They've never been cut apart,' he said, referring to the 16-page signatures still uncut, except for the first chapter.

"I repeated, "But what do you think?"

"'Oh, they'll change the history of the world alright,'" he said rather gravely.

Notes

1 From recordings made by Harold Hughes in anticipation of his writing a book.

Harold Hughes, circa 1964, meeting with mothers using the A.D.C. (Aid to Dependent Children) program. Hughes was a compassionate man who fought for the issues of the less fortunate. Photo: State Historical Society of Iowa, Des Moines.

CHAPTER TEN

Harold Hughes' Personal Characteristics

In his personal life, he is a man of intense feelings and compassion who can focus on broad, national issues involving human needs and rights without losing any of his personal intensity.[1]

NICK KOTZ AND JAMES RISSER

Harold Hughes had a complex personality and the authors of this book were challenged to do justice to his many facets.

A "giant," a "diamond in the rough," and a man with an "awesome power behind him." How does one adequately describe that individual? The challenge is to do justice to that imminent personality. In an attempt to adequately meet that challenge, we draw on the memories, observations, and experiences of members of his family, friends, and associates who worked with him. We also include some memories of individuals who knew Hughes well, as well as our own observations made over several years of our association with him.

A Committed Family Man and Friend

There is not a lot of evidence about Pack's (Hughes') family life while he was drinking, but family members relate that after he quit drinking, he was a devoted husband and father. Over the years he exhibited deep love for his family and worked hard to provide for them. He was very close to his mother and father and brother, Jesse. According to his daughter, Phyllis, he loved her mother, his first wife, Eva, and their children. His stepdaughters have fond memories of the mutual love and affection enjoyed between Hughes and his second wife, their mother, Julianne.

Many who knew him also knew Hughes as a very good friend. Pat Lingren, a friend from Ida Grove, who knew Hughes for many years said, "Hughes was the kindest, most gentle person I've ever known. He never met anyone who wasn't a friend ... I think the most important thing he would want to be remembered for is that he was a friend."[2]

His Mind

By his own admission, Hughes was not an "A" student in school. However, as an adult he possessed and demonstrated a brilliant mental capacity, was highly intelligent, and obviously very knowledgeable. One friend recalled that when Hughes was governor, he watched him listen to a room full of university presidents and other officials. One would think that Hughes might have been intimidated — but no. After listening, Hughes, with skill and clarity, summed up the conversation. To compliment his intelligence, he had an excellent memory. A former staff member recalled that Hughes could read through a speech once and deliver the speech with few references to the text. Another friend described him this way: "He (Harold) has a quick insightful mind and his capacity to learn is enormous. I've heard him listen to college professors, where one might suppose he'd be over his head, and then sum up everything getting right to the heart of the matter."[3]

"Robert Fulton, who served as Lieutenant Governor with Hughes in the 1960s, recalled Hughes' 'almost impeccable judgment.' His judgment gave him a clearer picture of the big picture than any other person I ever met."[4]

The governor was a man of superb executive skills. He could manage several complex projects or tasks simultaneously and keep them all organized. Close associates recall that Hughes liked to discuss big issues and to make decisions about big issues. That is not to say that he arrived at difficult solutions easily. He often brooded and struggled with problems before coming to a conclusion.

Some members of his staff recall that Hughes had great drive, determination, and executive ability.

His Emotions

"Hughes was a very compassionate man. He came from the wrong side of the tracks, and he was never afraid to talk about that. He always stood up for people who started from the bottom," said former Iowa Senator Tom Harkin about Hughes.

Hughes family members recalled that in his personal life he was a man of intense compassion and feeling. One friend observed that he had a very sensitive nature, which was usually kept well hidden, and that his feelings could easily be hurt by any form of unkindness. When the governor visited the economically depressed ghettos of Iowa's cities in the summer of 1967, he said, "I was humbled and was ashamed by suddenly realizing my own ignorance … reassessing morally my own position, I found myself bearing the guilt."[5]

Again, Governor Hughes' deep feelings were observed when he quietly, and without fanfare, visited Iowa's state prisons and mental hospitals. In the prisons he visited privately with every man on death row. He later related how moved he was by their stories. He pardoned some of those men whom he felt deserved to be pardoned.

In regard to Hughes, Kotz and Risser state, "It was his personal involvement in problems — you don't intellectualize about the victims of alcohol; you go out and help a victim turn loose of the bottle — that has marked Hughes' development as a public official. Always at the root is sensitivity to pain and suffering and an empathetic identification with sufferers and underdogs."[6]

His Style

Kotz and Risser describe the Governor in their article, *The Messiah from the Midwest?*: "The trademark of the Hughes political style has been an outspoken forthrightness on issues, presented with all the charismatic advantages of rugged good looks, imposing physique, deep bass voice, and compelling personal intensity. Yet his arrival at clear-cut positions on these issues has been a far more complex process than his strongly stated beliefs would indicate.[7]

"He [Hughes] is also a generalist, concerned and involved with the entire scope of human problems served by government. Much of his impact in the Senate has come in areas outside of the special confines of the committee assignments. His speeches convey a three-dimensional sense of contrast, contrasting with the brilliant but ad hoc styles of some of his colleagues.

"As governor, he was known for his blunt directness in cutting through non-essential matters to catalyze a solution. This quality has served him well as a senator. He has the courage to ask questions others may fear to ask and the ability to organize in short order the fragments of a meandering group discussion into a lucid whole."[8]

Close associates recall that Hughes was his own worst severe critic and that he was critical of anyone with whom he had close business, political, and personal relations.

Hughes' humanitarianism and commitment to the marginalized and disadvantaged was a quality that was obvious throughout his political life. His visits to Waterloo, Iowa, during racial crises and his commitment to the inmates in Iowa prisons and the patients in the mental hospitals exemplified that quality of concern and dedication.

"There were some skeptics who felt that Hughes possessed one of the worst attributes a politician could have — sincerity. Impassioned sincerity at that, he is obsessed with helping 'mankind.' But many others felt such qualities as dedication, sincerity, and humanitarianism are needed in today's troubled society and that Hughes could play the lighting rod role."[9]

And finally, there was his deep, resonating voice. When he was in the Senate, some of his colleagues considered him to be the most effective speaker in the Congress. Senator John Culver remembered, "There was an awesome power behind Harold Hughes. He could make the telephone book sound like Shakespeare."[10]

His Political Acumen

Several of the senator's qualities that are listed in the "style" section could also be identified as factors that contributed to his political mastery — for example, his transparency, frankness, and forthrightness. Iowans especially valued his openness and the fact that he spoke his mind. His ability to see through a "wide lens" and to articulate the focus and vision were definite political assets. His ability to persuade voters, colleagues, and senators was a huge quality that contributed to his political effectiveness.

After the so-called "Convocations on Crisis" held by the governor, he met with several groups of business and professional people around the state. Kotz and Risser wrote their description of Hughes: "Watching him eloquently and powerfully lecture to those businessmen about racism, one could sense that the 1958 'porpoise in the fishbowl' had burst free. The original, elemental qualities still produced the commanding leadership, but they now were refined, broadened, and under firm self-control. 'Once Hughes feels a problem,' as one observer puts it, he exhibits 'a combination of political pragmatism and social conscience in finding solutions.'"[11]

Hughes' self-confidence and his courage to take on controversial issues were recognized assets of a bright governor and U.S. senator. His stand on "alcohol by the drink" in Iowa, his opposition to the war in Vietnam, and his exposing of President Johnson's secret bombings in Vietnam exemplify these qualities.

The Compassion of a Mighty Man

In 1965, I [Evelyn Villines] was hired as Executive Secretary of the Governor's Committee on Employment of the Handicapped. After a couple of weeks in that position I received a message which stated, "The governor wishes to see you in his office, Thursday morning at ten o'clock." I was terrified. I arrived early and was told that I had a fifteen-minute appointment. I remember the office being cold, and the governor very tall. It seemed we talked about everything but my department. The appointment ended at twelve fifteen, over two hours later. From that day forward I knew I had a true friend.

On one occasion we were invited to participate in a Recognition Day for the Foster Grandparents Program at Glenwood State Hospital School. I was thrilled to ride there in the governor's car! Late in the afternoon we were invited to the cottage which housed the Foster Grandparent's Program. It was a dreary and rainy afternoon. As we walked into the living room the smell of fresh popcorn permeated the atmosphere. Governor Hughes walked over to a beautiful little girl who was strapped in her wheel chair. As he picked up her delicate little hand in his very large one, I remember the tears which streamed down his face. It was then I was made aware of the compassion of this "big man."[12]

Notes

1 From recordings made by Harold Hughes in anticipation of his writing a book.
2 *Ida County Courier*, October 30, 1996.
3 Ibid.
4 "Iowa Remembers Harold Hughes," *The Cedar Rapids Gazette*, October 25, 1996.
5 Kotz, Nick and Risser, James, "Messiah from the Midwest?," *The Washington Monthly*, May 1970.
6 Ibid.
7 Ibid.
8 Ibid.
9 MacPherson, "The Rise and Rise of Harold Hughes," *The Washington Post*, Sunday, December 20, 1979.

10 Ibid.

11 Kotz, Nick and Risser, James, "Messiah from the Midwest?," *The Washington Monthly*, May 1970.

12 Story told by Evelyn Villines, former Secretary of the Governor's Committee on Employment of the Handicapped.

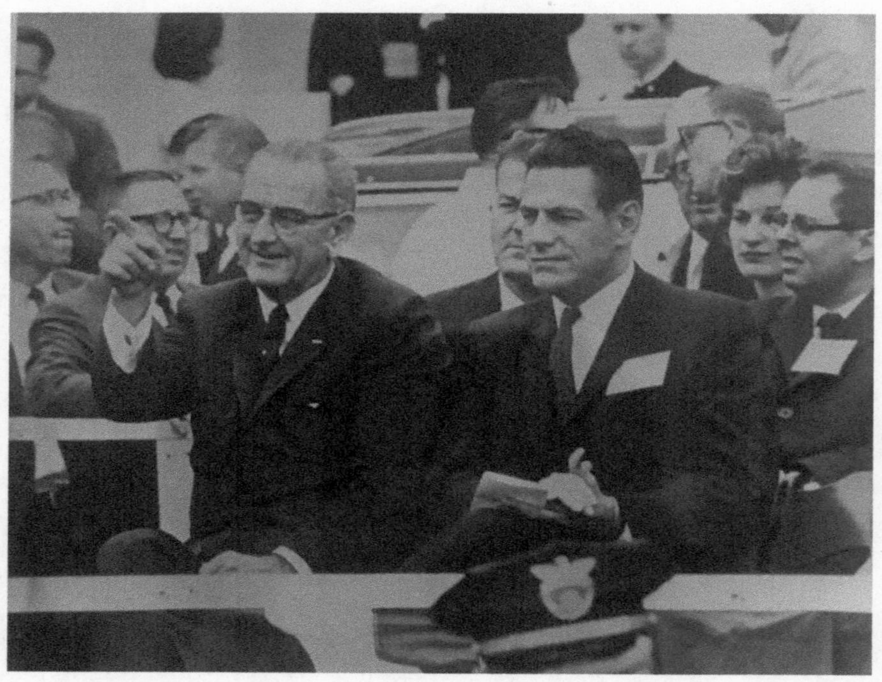

During his presidential campaign on October 7, 1964, President Lyndon Johnson points out to Governor Harold Hughes the big crowd all the way down Locust Street from their vantage point on the speaker's stand at the Statehouse in Des Moines.
Photo: Associated Press, State Historical Society of Iowa, Des Moines.

CHAPTER ELEVEN

The Turbulent 1960s and 1970s

Haynes Johnson describes the conflict in the streets of the (Democratic) convention. "I was an eye witness to the scene ... outside in the violence that descended after Chicago police took off their badges and waded into the charging crowds of protestors to club them to the ground. I can still recall the choking feeling from the tear gas hurled by police and the throngs of protestors gathering in parks and hotel lobbies.[1]

HAYNES JOHNSON

In order to accurately assess the leadership of Governor and Senator Hughes and his contributions to the State of Iowa and the nation, one must consider the decade in which he served. Hughes was elected governor in 1962 and served through 1968. He then served in the U.S. Senate from 1968 until 1975. Those years were marked by race riots, burned cities, the deaths of three revered leaders, the Vietnam War, and other horrific events.

The 1960s and early 1970s were a turbulent time for Iowa and especially for the nation. *U.S. News* called the 1960s "A Decade of Promise and Heartbreak" and a decade of extremes of transformation."

The young John F. Kennedy was elected president in 1960 and became a source of hope and optimism for the future, especially for younger people. That spirit of hope was lost with his untimely assassination in 1963.

In February 1960, four young black students occupied a "whites only" lunch counter at Woolworth's in Greensboro, North Carolina, setting off an avalanche of race riots in cities across the country. The Civil Rights Movement came to a boiling point in the 1960s and early 1970s. "Much of our memory of the Civil Rights Movement in the 1950s and 1960s is embodied in dramatic photographs, newsreels, and recorded speeches, which America encountered in daily papers and the nightly news. As the movement rolled across the nation, Americans absorbed images of hopeful, disciplined, and dedicated young people shaping their destinies. They were met with hostility, federal ambivalence and indifference, as well as mob and police violence. African Americans fought back with direct action protests and keen political organizing, such as voter registration drives and the Mississippi Freedom Democratic Party. The crowning achievement was the Civil Rights Act of 1964."[2]

During the Civil Rights Movement of the 1960s, Ella Baker, a civil rights activist, quoted, "Far more was at stake for these (civil rights) activists than changing the hearts of whites. When the sit-ins swept Atlanta in 1960, protestors' demands included jobs, healthcare, reform of the police and criminal justice system, education, and the vote."[3]

"In 1963 the March on Washington, most often remembered as the event at which Dr. King proclaimed his dream, was a demonstration for jobs and justice."[4]

President Kennedy was shot and killed in Dallas in 1963, raising the question whether Lee Harvey Oswald acted alone or was part of a conspiracy. Kennedy's brother, Robert, seeking nomination for president, was assassinated in 1968. Dr. Martin Luther King, Jr. was also shot and killed in Memphis in 1968. These horrific events triggered continuing riots in many cities across the country.

"The assassination of Martin Luther King, forty years ago today, was an event of singular importance, silencing one of the century's most profound and influential advocates for nonviolent change. But all too often what gets lost in the commemoration of King's death is the violence it unleashed around the country. It takes nothing away from King's greatness to suggest that when we look to that April day for historical import, we do a disservice by not going further to examine the broader consequences of James Earl Ray's gunshot.

"In only the strictest sense was King's death the cause of the riots. In Baltimore, Washington, Kansas City, and elsewhere, frustrations had been building for years. De facto segregation, workplace discrimination, police brutality, and immense poverty were the inescapable realities of ghetto life, and chafed against the postwar national rhetoric of consensus and progress. By the mid-1960s, ghettos around the country were tinderboxes, going off at the slightest provocation. And King's assassination was the greatest provocation possible.

"Over the course of the following week riots broke out in 125 cities nationwide. In many instances the National Guard was required to quell the violence. In Washington, Chicago and Baltimore, it took tens of thousands of regular Army soldiers and Marines. When they were over, some thirty-nine people were dead, more than 2,600 injured, and 21,000 arrested. The damages were estimated at sixty-five million dollars — about three hundred and eighty-five millions dollars today.

"But the real damage was rendered over a much longer term. First was the physical destruction. The riots literally burned out the centers of major American cities, and in their aftermath few investors, insurance companies, or businesspeople were willing to return. Dozens of inner cities, already under strain from the suburbs, simply collapsed, leaving in their wake a miasma of unemployment, crime, and poverty.[5]

"The unrest and violence affected many young Americans. The effect seemed especially bad because of the time in which they had grown up. By the middle 1950s most of their parents had jobs that paid well. They expressed satisfaction with their lives. They taught their children what were called 'middle class values.' These included a belief in God, hard work, and service to the country.

"Later, many young Americans began to question their beliefs. They felt that their parents' values were not enough to help them deal with the social and racial difficulties of the 1960s. They rebelled by letting their hair grow long and by wearing distinctive clothing. Their dissatisfaction was also strongly expressed in music."[6]

In an article in *Smithsonian* magazine, Haynes Johnson said, "The 1968 Democratic National Convention became a lacerating event, a distillation of a myriad of heartbreaks, assassinations, riots, and a breakdown in law and order that made it seem as if the country were coming apart. In its psychic imprint and its long-term political consequences, it eclipsed any other convention in American history, destroying faith in politics, in the political system, in the country, and in the constitution."[7]

Johnson describes the conflict in the streets of the convention. "I was an eyewitness to the scene ... outside in the violence that descended after Chicago police took off their badges and waded into the charging crowds of protestors to club them to the ground. I can still recall the choking feeling from the tear gas hurled by police and the throngs of protestors gathering in parks and hotel lobbies."[8]

At that convention Senator Hughes gave a speech nominating anti-war candidate Eugene McCarthy.

"The (Vietnam) war began in 1954 and continued until 1975. Massive protests were staged in Washington, D.C. and other cities by thousands of college students and others.

"The Vietnam War was a long and devisive conflict that pitted the communist government of North Vietnam against South Vietnam and its principal ally, the United States. The conflict was interrupted by the ongoing Cold War between the United States and the Soviet Union. A nuclear holocaust loomed over the country. More than three million people (including 58,000 Americans) were killed in the Vietnam War. Opposition to the Vietnam War bitterly divided Americans, even after President Nixon ordered the withdrawal of U.S. forces in 1973."[9]

Determined to exert their rights and to demand equal rights with men, the women of the nation staged demonstrations that became known as the Women's Liberation Movement.

Volumes could be written about the 60s and early 70s. Our purpose here is to emphasize the dynamic social and political climate that prevailed while Harold Hughes was governor and U.S. senator.

Notes

1 Johnson, Hayes, "The Bosses Strike Back," *The Smithsonian Magazine*, August 2008.
2 Janken, Kenneth R., *The Civil Rights Movement, 1919–1960's, Freedom's Story*, TeacherServe©, National Humanities Center, Washington, D.C., accessed October 2019.
3 Kleinfeldt, Rich, and Busby, Stan, *The Making of a Nation, A VOA Special English program about life in the U.S. in the 1960's.*
4 Janken, Kenneth R., *The Civil Rights Movement, 1919–1960's, Freedom's Story*, TeacherServe©, National Humanities Center, Washington, D.C., accessed October 2019
5 www.theguardian.com/commentisfree/2008/apr/04/thelegacyofthe1968riots
6 *American History: The 60's Become a Time of Social Revolution* (VOA Special English 2004-04-25; http://www.manythings.org/VOA/History/214.HTML.
7 Johnson, Hayes, "The Bosses Strike Back," *The Smithsonian Magazine*, August 2008.
8 Ibid.
9 American History: *The 60's Become a Time of Social Revolution* (VOA Special English 2007-04-25); http://www.manythings.org/VOA/History/214.HTML.

Julianne, Hughes' second wife, with Park Rinard, the man who was Hughes' teacher, his mentor, and a powerful and positive force behind him throughout his political career. Photo: Personal family photo used with permission of the Hughes family.

CHAPTER TWELVE

Political Mentor Park Rinard

He [Hughes] looked like a porpoise in a fishbowl,"
to Loveless' assistant, Park Rinard, who watched the giant man
in a lumberjack shirt sprawl out in his tiny two-dollar hotel room
and pour out his grievances against the "goddamn big truckers."
It was political love at first sight for idealistic and intellectual
Rinard, who sensed the very raw makings of a great politician.[1]

NICK KOTZ AND JAMES RISSER

One of Hughes' many assets was his ability to select very capable and outstanding people to work with him. Among those he chose was a man who had a huge influence on Hughes, Park Rinard. "Park made my life as a politician," Hughes said. "If there was any one person in the world who had an impact on my life, it was Park Rinard. I couldn't have done it without him."[2]

In a *Des Moines Register* article dated March 10, 1991, David Yepsen describes Rinard: "A gentle little man walks slowly through the U.S. Capitol, politely greeting doorkeepers and secretaries.

"His speech is slow and smooth, like the Scotch whiskey he loves. He likes tweed sport coats. Thick glasses magnify soft, dark eyes. He sits in his small office [in the U.S. Capitol] amid piles of books and papers, looking very much like the literature professor he almost became."

"Park Rinard, now seventy-nine, has played a large role behind the scenes in Iowa political life, shaping issues and counseling young politicians. Having kept a low profile in the shadows of some of the great figures of Iowa history," Senator Hughes said of Rinard, 'He is a quiet, peaceful, little man with a pipe and a core of steel and a heart of gold. He is the toughest man I ever met.'[3]

"Since 1957, when then-Governor Herschel Loveless asked him [Rinard] to move to Des Moines, Rinard has shaped the state's progressive and liberal agenda, providing the intellectual fuel and rhetoric for issues that still shape Iowa politics. For example, a speech Rinard wrote for Hughes is credited with breaking a logjam over creation of Iowa's community colleges, which today give thousands of people vocational training for better jobs on their first rung on the higher-education ladder."[4]

During the time that Hughes was running the Iowa Better Trucking Bureau, he was deeply concerned about the favoritism the Iowa State Commerce Commission was giving to the big trucking firms in the state. He decided to discuss his concerns with the governor, Herschel Loveless. Loveless heard his concerns and turned him over to his assistant, Park Rinard.

Hughes had no intention of entering politics, but his disgust with the unjust policies and practices of the Iowa State Commerce Commission drew him, as it were, into state politics. Many people supported Hughes during those years, but one individual highly influenced Hughes in regard to his entry into politics. That person became his teacher, his mentor, and a powerful and positive force behind him. That man was Park Rinard.

Park recalled that Loveless told him to look out for Hughes, and Park did. Hughes later related that Rinard "gave me a catechism class on government and how it worked."

Governor Loveless urged Hughes to run for a seat on the Iowa State Commerce Commission and instructed Rinard to coach him. Coach him he did, through two terms on the Commerce Commission and three two-year terms as governor.

James Larew in his *History of the A Party Reborn: The Democrats of Iowa, 1950–1974* said, "Hughes' fortunate access to prudent political counseling was an important key to his effective leadership. One man in particular — Park Rinard — ushered Hughes into the limelight."[5]

As Bobby Kennedy urged the Governor to run for the Senate, Hughes agreed to seriously consider that possibility. Hughes wanted to discuss the issue with his family. He also wanted to discuss it with his mentor and political advisor, Park Rinard. In fact, Hughes told Rinard that if he would not agree to going to the Senate with him, he wouldn't go. Obviously and fortunately, Rinard agreed.

Rinard's relationships with his bosses weren't always genial. "I got mad at Park a few times," Hughes says. "He thought he was a good campaign organizer. I didn't think he was worth a damn at that. I had a hard time getting him to keep his hands off the mechanics of campaign organization and stick to what I thought his real talents were, writing on issues."[6]

"While he has a very gentle nature, there's an inner toughness to him," [John] Culver recalls, speaking of Rinard. "He was very caring and yet at the same time he was very vigilant in terms of protecting his own turf. He was a tough little fighter. Rinard says he sometimes angered his bosses because the top duty of an aid to a public official is to tell him what he doesn't want to hear. If you can't do that then you aren't worth your salt."[7]

While many in politics today are there only temporarily to find lucrative business, lobbying, or consulting jobs," Culver says, "Rinard really is rare because of the extent to which he's dedicated his life to the service of what he believed in."[8]

U.S. Rep. Neal Smith hired Rinard after Culver's defeat in 1980, and at age seventy-eight [in 1990], Rinard remains an aide to the Altoona Democrat. "He's always in the background, and he's high quality," Smith says."[9]

Instrumental in persuading Hughes to run for the Iowa State Commerce Commission, which launched his political career, Rinard continued to loyally support him throughout his years in politics.

Notes

1 Kotz, Nick and Risser, James, "Messiah from the Midwest?," *The Washington Monthly*, May 1970.
2 Yepsen, David, "The Little Man Behind Some of Iowa's Greats," *Des Moines Register*, March 10, 1991.
3 Ibid.
4 Ibid.
5 Ibid.
6 Ibid.
7 Ibid.
8 Ibid.
9 Ibid.

Hughes at the Iowa State Commerce Commission at the end of his tenure as a member, here in 1962 with Red Skokie.
Photo: Personal photo, used with permission of the Hughes family.

CHAPTER THIRTEEN

A Run for the Iowa State Commerce Commission

His move into politics came when he saw what he felt were injustices in the state against small trucking firms he was representing at the time. Some friends challenged him to run for the Commerce Commission. He did in 1958 and won.

RUSSELL WILSON AND WILLIAM HEDLUND

Hughes organized and ran the Iowa Better Trucking Bureau for several years. As a result, he became interested in running for a seat on the Iowa State Commerce Commission. He said, "I ran into some disagreements with the director of the commission. After discussing those grievances with a friend, the friend said, "Harold, if you don't like the way the commission is being run, why don't you do something about it. A group of us will back you if you want to run for the commission post."

Hughes recorded, "I never dreamed of getting into politics. But I knew if I were going to do something significant about what I thought needed to be done in the commission, I had to get into the battle. My friends were Democrats and wanted me, a registered Republican, to run as a Democrat. I did. I won.

"That was the start of another whole new life. My life trend of doing everything to extremes didn't change when I got into politics. I worked day and night. I told people how I felt. And with my voice it came across loud and clear.

"I've been receiving commentaries on my voice all my life. Someone said I sounded like a 'bass tuba.' One person described me as 'a Mack truck with a voice like a volcano.' One reporter said I looked and sounded like Johnny Cash.

"One day another friend was in my office. 'Harold, being with you', he said timidly, 'is like being in a cage with a lion.' I am a large man, six feet three inches and 235 pounds. I'd prefer the 'tuba' image to the 'Mack truck' or 'lion ones.' That is probably because I played the bass tuba in high school.

"Speaking your mind can get you in trouble sometimes. I found myself getting deeper and deeper into the state politics the more I opened my mouth. Near the end of my four-year term as commissioner, I was approached by some men who asked me to run for governor. I knew I didn't have much of a chance because the state was so heavily Republican, but I accepted the bid.

"During the campaign, one of my opponents decided to dig out the dirty linen. On television he told people all over the state that I was an alcoholic. The next day I had a chance to reply. I admitted that he was right. I was an alcoholic, but I hadn't taken a drink for more than five years. Rather than hurt me, I believe those nights on television had a lot to do with my becoming governor.

"I served three terms as governor and then was elected to the United States Senate in 1968. "My work in AA and the church tapered off with the demands of the office."[1]

In a letter to Russ Wilson, Hughes discussed his new role as chairman of the Iowa State Commerce Commission: "My job here is a challenging one. It is very interesting in all of its diversity. As you may know, I was elected chairman of the commission and as a result must carry the burden of responsibility. We are making many changes and should have a very efficient staff and field force in another six months. It appears that the job I set out to do is at least within reach of accomplishment. This should have brought a great deal of satisfaction, but I find it lacking. The burdens of routine work here are tremendous. We have quite a number of hearings to sit through, which in the majority are boring. I find that in most cases it is not easy to draw a simple line between right and wrong or justice and injustice in those hearings."[2]

When Hughes decided to run for the Iowa State Commerce Commission, friends in Ida Grove gave him the money to run. Marva Benningsdorf of Ida Grove, daughter of Maudie and Marvin Rath, noted that her parents gave Hughes the money he needed to wage his campaign for the Iowa State Commerce Commission.

'I remember Mom saying that he hung his head and cried when they gave him the money. He knew it was all they had,' said Benningsdorf.[3]

A long-time friend of Hughes, Jim Lipton, recalled that in the 1950s, Hughes was a Republican. He was chosen to represent Ida County in the Republican State Convention, but Hughes' credentials to the convention were lost in a mix-up. He spent the day observing the convention from the gallery.

That experience and the fact that his friends urged him to change parties and run for governor caused Hughes to switch to the Democratic Party. He ran once in the primary in 1960 and lost, but ran again in 1962 and won.

Notes

1 From recordings made by Harold Hughes in anticipation of his writing a book.
2 From a personal letter to Russell and June Wilson.
3 *Ida Grove Courier*, Ida Grove, Iowa, Wednesday, October 30, 1996.

Governor Hughes with Montana Senator Mike Mansfield, with whom he shared a strong opposition to the Vietnam War. Photo: Official state photograph, used with permission of William Knapp.

CHAPTER FOURTEEN

Hughes is Elected Governor

[The new] Governor Hughes visited the state [mental] institutions and prisons and interviewed every man serving a life sentence. "Everywhere I looked, there was an overwhelming need to do something, urgently, now, not later. It was the most depressing experience of my life."

HAROLD HUGHES, AS TOLD BY THE AUTHORS

When Harold Hughes was elected governor in 1962, the only office to which he had previously been elected was the Iowa State Commerce Commission. Suddenly, he was to hold the highest office in the state. He said, "The biggest shock of being elected governor was that it was overwhelming immediately." He had thought the avalanche of activity would not come until after the inauguration. Hughes said, "The campaign is about issues and all your energy and efforts are on the issues and not on gearing up for taking the reins of government. Election night, when the final results are in, the press and media are overwhelming, wanting you for statements and TV appearances. This went on until about three am.

"When we finally got to sleep, the telephone rang and Eva answered it. A man's voice said 'You tell your husband I am going to kill him.' The voice continued 'I'm dead serious.' Eva asked who it was. 'It doesn't matter who this is. I mean business, I'm going to kill your husband.' She hung up and told me what was said and I said, 'it's just some prank.'

"Then, I thought maybe we had better call the police. He might be outside the house. Eva picked up the phone to call the police and the man had not hung up and was still on the line. He wouldn't hang up and again said 'I'm going to kill your husband.'

"We had only one phone, so I suggested Eva go next door and use their phone to call the police. Many different things raced through our minds as we contemplated what to do. We picked up the phone again and the line was open so we called the police to report the call. The police didn't send anyone out and said that it is some sort of crank call and they get them all the time. Well, frankly, it scared the hell out of us. That's the first time in my life that happened.

"The next day the press and media were conducting interviews. People wanted to talk about their ideas for legislation and every lobbying group wanted time to talk with the governor-elect. Budget hearings for state departments would begin on December 1. Governor Norman Erbe would be conducting the hearings and I would be delivering the budget message to the 1963 General Assembly. Governor Erbe invited me to his office and we had a frank discussion. The governor offered to let me sit in on the hearings. I have nothing but the highest respect for the way Norman Erbe turned over the reins of government to me when I was elected. It was done with dignity, and I think concern for the best interests of the people of Iowa.

"The requests for jobs were also overwhelming. Those who had worked for former Governor Herschel Loveless and released under Erbe's Republican administration wanted back in under the Hughes administration. I needed staff to help work on all the tasks before me but I had no staff. When the same party transitions to the office, secretarial help and office space are probably made available. I didn't know that a governor-elect from the opposite party had no funds to set up an office and hire staff. Friends provided limited office space and volunteers helped until the inauguration, at which time the office of the governor became available. The boards and commissions in state government required appointments be made."[1]

In 1965 Governor Hughes recommended funding for a new governor to assist in the transition of the office and an appropriation was passed to facilitate that important function. The need to know what the functions of each board was, and finding people to fill the positions was a difficult task. There were social affairs and media demands. In his recordings, Hughes said "All of these responsibilities and demands of a newly-elected governor were unknown to me."

Governor Hughes faced a number of significant challenges. The state had limited funds and no surplus. The need for more funding for state buildings and universities was called for. The penal institutions were in need of remedial services for inmates and money for custodial staff.

Governor Hughes visited the state institutions and prisons and interviewed every man serving a life sentence. The pay structure for staff at the penal and mental health facilities was low. After the visits, Hughes said "The workers were either the most dedicated people in the world or … people who couldn't find any other job."

"Everywhere I looked, there was an overwhelming need to do something, urgently, now, not later. It sounds like turmoil, and it was, but it was the greatest experience of my life. Plus, at times, it was the most depressing experience of my life."[2]

As a newly elected governor, Hughes found many problems and challenges that the campaign for governor didn't address. It was the beginning of his time in the office of governor and the learning experience continued for months.

Throughout the rest of the book short personal stories are interspersed. They are not meant to be chronological, but are simply interesting stories that came from Hughes and the authors and shed even more light into his complex life.

A Hunting Trip to Yucatan

While serving as governor, Hughes traveled to Yucatan on a hunting trip with Gene Kieffer, his friend and publicity and marketing advisor. They went to hunt big game in the dense jungle.

While they were there, Hughes' father died. He needed to return home to the states immediately.

As Hughes told Russ Wilson, "A small, single-engine plane was sent to pick us up and take us to the nearest commercial airport.

The pilot landed on the tiny airstrip that had been carved out of the jungle. Tall trees and jungle underbrush lined the strip on all sides. We loaded our gear, backpacks, and guns in the small craft. I'm sure we were over the load limit for the tiny plane. The pilot did not understand English so we couldn't communicate with him or he with us! When we were loaded, the pilot taxied as close to the end of the dirt runway as possible. Then he revved up the engine, checked magneto one, then magneto two, then idled the engine down, clasped his hands, and bowed his head in prayer. After a minute or two he pushed the throttle to the max and we barely made it over the trees."[3]

White Tie and Tails

On several occasions while Russ Wilson served on the Iowa State Board of Control, the governor's aide would call and tell Wilson that Hughes wanted him to travel to Washington, D.C. or some other destination with him on state business. On one occasion, Hughes and Wilson arrived in Washington, D.C. about four o'clock in the afternoon. Hughes had been invited to attend the Gridiron Club, a prestigious annual gathering of the elite in Washington. It was a coveted honor to be invited to the event.

Wilson recalls, "We went to Hughes' hotel room where he kicked off his shoes and laid down on the bed to rest. In a few minutes he called Nick Kotz, the *Des Moines Register's* Washington correspondent, who Hughes knew when he was assigned to the Iowa Capitol beat in Des Moines.

"Kotz was nearby and in a few minutes knocked on the door of the room. After some small talk, Kotz said to the Governor, 'How do you look in your white tie and tails?' Hughes, somewhat dismayed, reached into his briefcase and pulled the invitation from its envelope. Sure enough, the invitation specified 'white tie and tails.' Hughes had brought his tuxedo, but not a 'white tie and tails' outfit.

"Fortunately, Kotz knew of a clothier a mile or so from the hotel, and called him. It was nearly five o'clock, closing time, but the two owners agreed to wait for the governor. In a flurry of activity, Hughes, Kotz, and Wilson went to the clothier where the two brothers scrambled to outfit the six foot three inch, 235 pound Hughes, in 'white tie and tails.' With the garments in a couple of large plastic bags, Hughes and Wilson returned to the hotel.

By the time they reached the hotel, it was time to get dressed for the big event. For those who do not know, 'white tie and tails' is the most formal of all dress codes and typically associated with presidential dinners and royal affairs. It involves a somewhat complicated arrangement of clothing including a cummerbund, a wing collared shirt, a white bowtie and cuff links, and everything has to be arranged in the right sequence.

Neither Hughes nor Wilson had ever worn nor helped another person put on this outfit, but through trial and error, they got Hughes dressed. Then Hughes, a bit uncertain about whether he was dressed correctly or not said, "Wilson, go down and stand in the hall where the event is being held and check out the other men as they come in. See if I look like them and come back up and tell me."

Wilson went down and stood in the corridor and watched the vice president, several congressmen and other dignitaries walk in, and checked them out. He returned to tell Hughes that he looked okay and Hughes went to the meeting.[4]

Even though he was expected to rise to the occasion on more formal occasions like this, to his neighbors at home in Iowa, he remained the same down-home Iowan. Neighbors living near the governor's mansion remembered one morning when they looked out and saw Hughes in his bathrobe and slippers chasing his English Setter, Mike, down the street. In spite of losing his slippers in the mud, he finally caught the incorrigible dog and returned him to the mansion. A friend of Russ Wilson's daughter who lived near the governor's mansion when she was a child remembers finding the dog wandering the neighborhood one day. She and her cousin simply walked up to the back door of the mansion with the dog on a leash, knocked, and were greeted by Hughes in his bathrobe and a huge head of disheveled hair, obviously having just risen from bed. He greeted the girls and thanked them for returning his dog. Those were certainly different days.

Notes

1 From recordings made by Harold Hughes in anticipation of his writing a book.
2 Ibid.
3 As remembered by the book's author, Russell Wilson
4 As remembered by the book's author, Russell Wilson

Hughes is welcomed in his hometown of Ida Grove, Iowa, soon after being elected governor in 1962. Photo: Courtesy Conley Wolterman, historic archives, Ida Grove, Iowa.

Governor Hughes and wife Eva, in a 1962 homecoming to their hometown, Ida Grove, Iowa. Photo: Courtesy Conley Wolterman, historic archives, Ida Grove, Iowa.

Governor Hughes in his office on inauguration day 1965, after being elected to a second term as Iowa's governor in 1964. Photo: Official state photo.

Hughes and his wife Eva, on his inauguration day as governor in 1965, with their family: (left to right) daughters Carol, Phyllis, and Connie, and Connie's husband Dennis holding their daughter, Tracy. Photo: Official state photo, used with permission of the Hughes family.

Governor Hughes signing his first bill as governor, January 28, 1963. From 1962–1968, Hughes signed many new laws for the citizens of Iowa.
Photo: WHO News photo, State Historical Society of Iowa, Des Moines

CHAPTER FIFTEEN

Accomplishments as Governor

Surveys indicated that liquor was being sold openly and freely in over 75 counties. … The only way to correct it was to face it squarely.

HAROLD E. HUGHES

Liquor by the Drink

Prior to 1963, it wasn't legal to buy liquor-by-the-drink in Iowa. In his recording, Hughes recalled that the subject became an issue in his 1962 campaign for governor. He said a group of so-called advisors discussed the liquor-by-the-drink issue and their consensus was that it had been political death for candidates for four years, and that he should not touch the subject with a proverbial ten-foot pole. The group advised him to avoid controversy by saying he would enforce the law. Some of the group had the impression that Hughes agreed to follow that advice, but he didn't agree. The aspiring governor felt the issue was one that had to be faced squarely, and his close advisor, Park Rinard, agreed.[1]

Hughes went on to say, "We were not trying to legalize liquor or to make liquor freer for consumption. Our objective was to end the hypocrisy and the total disrespect for the law."[2]

Hughes thought the issue of liquor-by-the-drink was out of proportion in the campaign, as there were more important issues to be addressed. He said, "About the only thing I was remembered for in the campaign was being the first man to come out for liquor-by-the-drink. It was an emotional issue of the day and time. I don't know whether another man or woman doing the same thing would have had the same effect or not."[3]

The press wrote that Hughes was a recovered alcoholic and a Methodist lay speaker, and that gave him credentials for advocating liquor-by-the-drink. Hughes disagreed with that logic. He said, "Surveys indicated that liquor was being sold openly and freely in over seventy-five counties. Teenagers could buy liquor, bootleggers were running wild, and everyone was laughing at the law. The only way to correct it was to face it squarely. Everyone has forgotten that I would dry up the state if we didn't legalize liquor. I put every enforcement officer that I had to closing the bars and bootleggers down. You can't succeed 100%, but I think I had 98% of them closed down, including country clubs, veterans' clubs, and everything else we could legally shut down. I would have continued to enforce the law."[4]

"Hughes tapped a latent Iowa majority who desired a progressive state image. They were tired of jokes about the little old lady from Dubuque and about key clubs and wanted more from their political leaders than cautious mediocrity."[5]

"Although the legislature was controlled by the Republicans in both houses, the 1963 General Assembly passed the law to provide liquor by the drink. The bill was debated late in the evening and was passed in the House by a vote of sixty-eight to forty and the vote in the Senate was twenty-seven to twenty-three. Senator Jack Kibbie and two friends of Governor Hughes went down to the governor's office after passage of the law and Hughes was sitting with his feet up on the desk and had been listening to the debate. Hughes was happy with the results."[6]

"For the man who was the force behind the change — Governor Harold E. Hughes — the bill's passage was 'statesmanship of the highest order.'"[7]

Harold Hughes' leadership on the change in the liquor-by-the-drink law in Iowa was the beginning of his leadership on many future issues including the abolishment of the death penalty.

The Death Penalty Abolished

"In the 1962 campaign for Governor, Harold Hughes called for the abolishment of capital punishment. After winning the election in November, he recommended legislation to end the death penalty in the General Assembly in 1963. Hughes had read studies that capital punishment did not deter crime. His religious beliefs reinforced his opposition. The legislative session in 1963 ended without any action on the death penalty issue."[8]

Later that year, a doctor in Dubuque, Iowa, was kidnapped and taken into Illinois and killed. The killer was apprehended and charged with a federal crime as he had crossed a state line. He was sentenced to death and because the abduction began in Iowa, the execution would be conducted in Iowa. The death penalty in Iowa was by hanging.[9]

"The Governor was powerless to commute the sentence of death as it was a federal crime. He appealed to President John Kennedy to spare the man's life. The President told Hughes he had nothing on which to base a commutation considering the law and the mood in the country. Hughes replied, "I have to accept your decision, but my conscience totally rejects it."[10]

"The man to be executed was being held in the Fort Madison Penitentiary. The chaplain at the facility informed the prisoner that Governor Hughes had tried to stop his execution. The chaplain sent Hughes a note from the condemned person, Leo Figura. 'Dear Mr. Governor: I don't understand why a man like you cares about me, but I thank you for what you tried to do. While here, I have come to believe in Jesus Christ and now I will soon know more about him. Thank you, Leo Figura.'"[11]

Leo Figura was executed at dawn. Dwight Jensen, Executive Assistant to Governor Hughes said later that morning Hughes asked his secretary and Dwight to leave the Capitol Building and go for coffee. Hughes wanted to get away from the phone calls and the press wanting his comments about the execution. It was a time he needed to pause and reflect on his feelings.[12]

"Governor Hughes was concerned about the penal system. Many lifers were not being considered for a commutation or receiving one. He asked for a list of lifers who had been in prison for over fifteen years. Hughes went to the Fort Madison Penitentiary and interviewed each one of them. The first lifer became very emotional during the interview. He had appealed to all the governors during his forty years in prison and had never heard a word in reply. After the interviews, Hughes began the process of commutation for that lifer. It took three months for the paperwork and the review by the state agencies involved before the governor could proceed with the commutation. Papers for the release of the inmate had to go to the hospital as the man had suffered a heart attack. The day after the man received the notification of his release, he died."[13]

"News of the commutation spread among the inmates and resulted in a riot at Fort Madison. Some prisoners barricaded themselves in a cellblock and burned the laundry. Once prison officials were able to talk with the rioters, the prisoners had many grievances and wanted to talk with the governor. Against the advice of prison officials, Hughes agreed to talk with the men. A phone hookup was arranged and Hughes stated his conditions for the talk. They had to give up their weapons, leave the barricade, and suffer any penalties for their actions. The prisoners agreed to the terms of the governor. They had eighteen grievances. Hughes told them he would consider ten. The grievances included food, work conditions, free time, and library privileges. Hughes worked on solutions to the issues. A special committee of inmates was created to bring their concerns to the State Director of Corrections.

There were no more riots. "Communication, I was learning, was the key to understanding."[14]

The death penalty was abolished in 1965. The Iowa Legislature took the action after long debate to end the long-term law.

One of Hughes' remarkable qualities was his lifelong commitment to responding to another person in trouble. In the following story, Russ Wilson recalls one such time, when the governor responded to another's call for help.

A Meeting with an Alcoholic

While Russ Wilson was a member of the Board of Control, the Hughes family invited the Wilsons to dinner at the governor's mansion. After dinner, the group was visiting in the living room when the phone rang.

Wilson recalls that the phone call was from a friend of Hughes who was an alcoholic and who was having a difficult time. He had arrived home from London that day. He was alone and struggling with his addiction. He asked if Hughes would come and be with him for a while.

Hughes got his coat, invited Russ to go along, and the two drove to the south side of town to meet with the man. After spending more than an hour with him, the friend was feeling better, and the two returned to the mansion.

That is only one of hundreds of times Harold Hughes responded to the call of an alcoholic who was in trouble. No matter the circumstances, what he was doing, or who the troubled person was, Hughes would respond to help. Elsewhere in this book is the story of how he stayed with a senior senator in Washington, also an alcoholic, who was considering suicide. Hughes spent several hours with the senator until he was through his crisis.

While Hughes served as U.S. senator, he helped many alcoholics or couples who were having trouble with their marriages. Following is a classic story of his work with a fellow senator. [15]

The Good Samaritan

"On the first day in the United States Senate, while waiting to be sworn in, Harold Hughes felt a hand on his shoulder. A voice behind him said 'I don't like you.' Hughes couldn't understand why he was disliked by a man he did not know. The individual, another senator, said, 'It is because you nominated Gene McCarthy for President.' The senator later apologized for his remarks. Later at home, Hughes was called by that senator's staff assistant asking him to come to the senator's office on Capitol Hill. The senator had been drinking and was slumped on his desk. There was the smell of bourbon in the room.

Hughes thought of how many times earlier in his life that his wife, Eva, had seen him in a similar condition. The drunk senator said killing himself was the only way out of his frustration and bitterness at what he felt were unfair accusations by peers and the betrayal of a trusted aid. Hughes stayed with him until three am. The two men became friends as Hughes helped him with his drinking problem and the senator assisted Hughes in learning the rules and procedures of the senate."[16]

Many years later after both senators were deceased, Senator Chris Dodd of Connecticut was in Iowa City on a speaking engagement. After the speech, Dwight Jensen, who had been Executive Assistant to Governor Hughes and Press Secretary in the Senate office in the early years, approached Senator Dodd and introduced himself. Senator Dodd said, "Harold Hughes saved my dad's life."[17]

Patrick Deluhrey, one of the Senator's staff, "remembered that one night Senator Hughes was called by a good friend of a congressman asking Hughes to come and help the congressman who was with a woman friend in his apartment and very inebriated. Hughes went and asked the woman to go into the other room. He sat with the congressman and talked about how he had experienced alcoholism in his life and what it does to oneself and one's family."[18]

"Harold Hughes would drop everything he was doing to respond to a call from a person with an alcohol problem. His own history of alcoholism was important in relating with the person about the problem."[19]

One of the truly great contributions that Hughes made was that he openly and transparently admitted his alcoholism history. Prior to that time, alcoholism was kept under wraps.

Notes

1 From recordings made by Harold Hughes in anticipation of his writing a book.
2 Ibid.
3 Ibid.
4 Ibid.
5 Kotz, Nick, and Risser, James, *Messiah from the Midwest?, The Washington Monthly*, May 1970.
6 Kibbie, Jack, former State Senator, Emmetsburg, Iowa, October, 2017.
7 Herrington, Jerry, *Iowa's Last Bottle: Governor Harold E. Hughes and the Liquor-by-the-Drink Conflict*, Annals of Iowa, Volume 76, Number 1, 2017 (Editor's Note: Good history of the issue.)
8 Schneider, Dick, *Harold E. Hughes, The Man from Ida Grove*, Chosen Books, Lincoln, Virginia, 1979.
9 Ibid.
10 Ibid.
11 Ibid.
12 Jensen, Dwight, Iowa City, Iowa, 2017.
13 Schneider, Dick, *Harold E. Hughes, The Man from Ida Grove*, Chosen Books, Lincoln, Virginia, 1979.
14 Ibid.
15 As remembered by the author, Russell Wilson
16 Ibid.
17 Jensen, Dwight, Iowa City, Iowa, 2017.
18 Deluhrey, Patrick, Des Moines, Iowa, 2018.
19 Schneider, Dick, *Harold E. Hughes, The Man from Ida Grove*, Chosen Books, Lincoln, Virginia, 1979.

Governor Harold E. Hughes with his 1967 staff.
(Seated from left) Bill Hedlund, Governor Hughes and Dwight Jensen.
(Standing from left) Dick Nehring, Wade Clark, Les Holland, Martin Jensen and Ed Campbell.
Photo: Official state photograph.

CHAPTER SIXTEEN

More Accomplishments as Governor

Legislation creating area vocational-technical schools in Iowa was passed by both houses and Governor Hughes signed it. This landmark law provided a new form of post high school education in Iowa. Governor Hughes proposed the concept and the legislature refined it.[1]

FORMER IOWA SENATOR JACK KIBBIE

Creation of Vocational-Technical Schools in Iowa

"In his campaign for reelection in 1964, Governor Harold Hughes recommended the establishment of four vocational-technical training schools in Iowa. The four schools would be state-supported and state-operated. Hughes was reelected with a great majority over his opponent in a Democratic landslide. Democrats won the five elective state offices, six of the seven congressional seats, and a majority of both houses of the Iowa General Assembly.[2]

"A study of the entire educational system in Iowa was passed by the legislature in 1959. The Gibson Report contained a section about merging vocational-technical schools and the arts and sciences curriculum to create area schools. The Senate Education Committee held many meetings in the 1965 session studying and debating proposals in the Gibson Report and the recommendation of Governor Hughes for the establishment of vocational-technical schools in Iowa. The Committee sent a bill to the floor that provided for county boards of education to be merged to form a district of three counties. The formed district could levy a tax of one mill on property to be used for the operation of the school. In addition, the public could vote for a one mill tax for brick and mortar."[3] The legislation was passed by both houses and signed by Governor Hughes. This landmark law provided a new form of post high school education in Iowa. Governor Hughes proposed the concept. The legislature refined it.

Republicans regained the majority in the House of Representatives in the 1966 election. Democrats held on to the Senate. Governor Harold E. Hughes was reelected, as was Lt. Governor Robert Fulton. House Republicans in the 1967 session made every effort to undo some of the actions of the 1965 General Assembly. "The House passed a bill to repeal the one mill levy for the brick and mortar of the area schools. The Senate passed a bill restoring the one mill levy. A conference committee was appointed and Senator Jack Kibbie and Representative Charles Grassley were co-chairs. An agreement was reached after numerous meetings, which reduced the millage rate for both operations and buildings from one mill to three-fourths of a mill. Both houses of the legislature passed the amended bill. Governor Hughes signed it into law. Many attempts have been made to change the tax rate over the last fifty years, but it still stands."[4]

"For several years the State Board of Regents (which oversees the state universities and the schools for the blind and the deaf) was opposed to teaching any arts and science courses at the community colleges. That changed over time, and the transfer of credit hours from community colleges has become a great feeder system for the four-year institutions. The community colleges provide an opportunity for students to obtain two years of higher education at a lower cost. The vocational-technical programs offer a variety of training for those individuals wanting a trade. Many large corporations (i.e. General Motors and John Deere) and many small businesses work with the community colleges in training the workforce. The full-time enrollment at the community colleges in 2015 was 100,000 and part-time and Saturdays was more than double that. Jack Kibbie said, 'The program would not have happened without Governor Harold Hughes.'"[5]

1967 General Assembly Tax Debate, Meeting with Legislative Leaders

The 1965 legislature was highly productive. It passed constitutional amendments, abolished capital punishment, approved the establishment of four new vocational-technical schools, authorized withholding of state income taxes from paychecks, and increased state aid to local schools by fifteen million dollars per year. "The legislature realized that a revision of the state tax structure was long overdue. An appropriation of $50,000 for a study of the Iowa tax structure passed. The study was to be completed during the interim and make recommendations to the General Assembly in 1967."[6]

Dr. James Papke, an economist at Purdue University, was employed to conduct the study. After a thorough study, the findings and recommendations were presented to the governor, leaders of both parties, and financial experts in the state prior to the convening of the 1967 General Assembly. The study was made available to all members of the legislature at the start of the session.

The tax study was a starting point for consideration and debate, but once the 1967 session began there were many difficulties in getting any proposed legislation agreed upon. The tax issue dragged on and was bogged down in both houses of the General Assembly. Very late in the session, Governor Hughes called the leadership of both parties to a meeting in his office. The Lieutenant Governor, Speaker of the House, majority and minority leaders of each house, and the chairman and ranking member of the Appropriations Committee as well as the Ways and Means Committee of each house were in attendance. Each person voiced his thoughts and opinions on taxes in Iowa. The agreement of ideas and what might be done was interesting. The discussion was free and open among the participants as there was no press present, no interest groups, and no citizens in the room. A variety of issues that affected many different areas of the tax structure were discussed. "The focus was on basic matters of school aid, equalization of property assessments, an increase in the sales tax, and a tax on services. Agreement on equalization of property assessments in the counties was essential if increased funds were going to go for school aid and agricultural land tax credits. It was agreed by all present they would support the tax package."[7]

"Because the session was so long, the leaders of both houses agreed to bypass the regular committee system of approving bills and take the proposed tax bills directly to the floor. Debate and opposition to the sales tax increase and addition of the tax on services was intense. The equalization of assessment for property tax purposes was acceptable. It had been hoped to adjourn by late Friday night, June 30, but a final package wasn't passed until Sunday, July 2, 1967 — the 175th day of the legislative session. The final laws increased sales tax to three percent and added to services, other increases were on cigarettes and beer. All real and personal property would be assessed at twenty-seven percent of its fair and reasonable value beginning January 1, 1968."[8]

"The tax package was not popular on many fronts. Newspaper editorials, for the most part, were strongly opposed. The Centerville *Iowegian* stated 'Never in all history has such a major piece of legislation been handed out under such cloak and dagger techniques… little wonder the governor and the Legislature are being soundly criticized.' A positive editorial in the Boone *News-Republican* said '… to the extent that the new tax bill provides property tax relief in the operation of public schools, it will be welcome. Iowa taxpayers may find that the taxes added amount to almost as much as the property tax relief.'"[9]

The 1966 election resulted in a Republican majority in the House of Representatives and a Democratic majority in the Senate. "Divided control actually opened the way to passage of some of the most far-reaching legislation in Iowa's history — legislation that neither party had been able to put through in recent years when it alone controlled both houses."[10]

Legislative leaders of both parties worked to bring about a bipartisan effort on the tax package. Lt. Governor Robert Fulton and Speaker of the House Maurice Baringer were instrumental in the negotiations during the final days of the 1967 session.

Governor Hughes sent an adjournment message in a letter to the members of the General Assembly, who had been in a long and arduous session for 175 days. The letter said in part: "The cardinal accomplishment of this session was your courage in meeting the long-standing need for major tax revision ... The extensive tax program enacted to finance the massive property tax relief represents, on your part, conscientious effort to equalize the tax load among all segments of our society. There isn't a citizen who won't carry his proportionate share of the tax load, nor is there a citizen who won't share, in some measure, the relief from the repressive taxes on property."[11]

After the legislators went home following the 1967 session, the media continued to criticize the governor on the tax law. The press was taxed in the new law. Hughes felt that was some of the reason for their criticism. All those involved at the meeting in the governor's office had agreed to support the plan, which they did in passage of the law. But once the legislators went home, it was easier for the press to question the governor. "Hughes felt he had fulfilled his part of the bargain, and the responsibility should have been a shared burden. Regardless of the aftermath, Hughes felt the passage of the tax package had been long needed and was good for the state."[12] By bringing the legislative leaders to meet on the tax structure in Iowa, Hughes provided the initiative to pass the new legislation.

The Amish School Controversy

The area around Hazelton, Iowa, where The Old Order Amish lived, had been part of the Oelwein school district since 1962. At times, problems had occurred between the school district and some Amish who did not employ certified teachers. One day in late 1965, the school bus from the Oelwein school district arrived at one of the Amish schools to transport the students to the public school in Hazleton. The students ran into the nearby cornfield rather than boarding the bus. The incident was recorded by a Waterloo television station and became a national news story.

Governor Hughes was concerned and felt the Amish should be able to educate their children while following their way of life and religious beliefs. The governor met with the Amish fathers of students from two schools involved and the Oelwein School Board to learn more about the problem. The Amish said they could not pay for certified teachers at their private schools. The most serious objection was the integration of their children with those in the public schools. Meeting with the school board, Hughes told the board he realized the difficult position they were in and he was there to work with them. He understood they had to uphold the law requiring certified teachers in the schools. He said, "I want to be your 'shock absorber' and take the pressure off of you." Hughes suggested a temporary solution to cover the time until the legislature met. He would then recommend a permanent solution.[13]

"Governor Hughes met several times with the Amish fathers and the Oelwein School Board on a temporary plan to obtain private funds to pay for certified teachers for the ensuing year and the next year until the next legislative session. Overcoming objection from the Amish that they could not accept charity, an agreement was reached. The School Board would receive the private funds and select and pay the teachers in the two schools, since they would then be part of the public school system. The building housing the Amish students would be leased by the school board for a nominal fee. The governor suggested a statement of understanding be drafted and signed by the Oelwein School Board and the Amish. It was signed February 1, 1966, in Hazelton, Iowa."[14]

"Funding was obtained in a grant from the Danforth Foundation in St. Louis, Missouri, for $15,000 for the remainder of the 1965–66 school year and for the entire 1966–67 school year."[15]

Hughes announced the signing of the agreement. "I felt it was the responsibility of those of us outside the Amish community to exercise the utmost patience and good faith in communicating to good people of this minority group that we prize and cherish their religious freedom and their right to live their own way."[16]

There was opposition to the settlement even among other Amish who were sending their children to public schools. Other critics held that the Amish should abide by the law and no exemptions should be granted. An editorial by station WMT said in part, "The agreement ... contains a comprise ... the Amish would have certified teachers in the rural atmosphere the Amish hold in such high regard ... and has become possible through the mediation of Governor Hughes and concessions made by both sides."[17]

Governor Hughes followed through with his commitment to recommend permanent legislation to the legislature to end the Amish school controversy. First he appointed a Special Committee to examine the question of education of Amish children in Iowa. "The recommendation of the Special Committee was to exempt private schools from the state law and permit the State Superintendent of Public Instruction and the State Board of Education to have the discretion to exempt such schools. It was agreed the committee's proposal had a better chance of passage than the governor's recommendation of state aid to pay for the teacher in the Amish schools. The Amish fathers approved the proposed legislation and expressed appreciation for Governor Hughes' good deeds and his kind and personal concern for them."[18]

Senate File 785 passed the General Assembly. It "provided that local congregations of a recognized church or religious denomination having been ten or more years in Iowa which profess principles or tenets differing from the standards of the educational law can file with the Superintendent of Public Instruction for exemption from the standards for two years. Proof of achievement in the basic skills is essential for renewal of the exemption by the State Superintendent and the State Board."[19]

The Amish school controversy and the process by which it was resolved are an example of Hughes' leadership. He involved himself in what was considered a politically hazardous situation. His ability to bring people together, his dedication to equitable solutions, and ultimately his compassion and respect for people, culminated in a successful resolution. The governor worked long and hard with both sides to help them to come to a mutually acceptable resolution.

Hughes and the Vietnam War

In the early years of the conflict, Harold Hughes supported the military action in Vietnam. However, opposition to the war began to build within him. Senators Gene McCarthy and Robert Kennedy were openly critical of the war and of President Johnson's policy in Southeast Asia.

"Ten governors [including Hughes] were going to Japan in the fall of 1966 on an exchange visit. President Johnson asked them to stop in Vietnam for an inspection tour of South Vietnam. The tour was structured to show the progress being made in the war effort. Returning home, Hughes began to have serious concerns about the conflict and the progress of the war."[20]

Some people in 1966 were suggesting that Hughes run for the United States Senate. He decided to run for a third term as governor as there were more things he wanted to accomplish in Iowa. The 1966 election resulted in Democrats losing many congressional seats and Democratic governors. There was a strong, growing discontent with the war.

"The National Democratic Governor's Conference held a meeting in December 1966 after the election. The governors agreed the loss of Democrats in November was the result of Johnson's war policy. The news that the governors were placing the blame on the president hit the media outlets. The anti-war factions were excited by the development, while the supporters of the president were angry."[21]

"President Johnson invited the Democratic governors to the Texas White House in January, 1967. Only twelve governors attended as others did not want to encounter an angry president. Each governor was given the opportunity to voice their view. The president took

Hughes into another room and angrily told him he had hurt the party and the president by his remarks in December.

"Hughes had been the spokesman for the Democratic governors. A more amicable time followed lunch and on leaving, Johnson and Hughes talked to the press before the governors left. Hughes said 'We had made peace and expressed strong support for the administration. Though I could not bring myself to withdraw my statement at White Sulphur Springs, I pointed out we all had agreed to be together for a common purpose.'"[22]

A few years later in Washington, Ernie Olson, a member of the Secret Service, told author Bill Hedlund about a time he remembered at the Johnson Ranch. Olson was at the gate to the ranch when a fellow agent called him and told him to come to the house immediately. When he arrived and looked in the window, LBJ and Hughes were facing each other and engaged in a spirited discussion. The two agents said they had never before seen anybody stand up to the president. Hughes was as big and tall as Johnson. As a result of the incident, Iowa never received much federal assistance after that.

As the governor approached the end of his third term in late 1967, he was asked by the press and others if he planned to run for another term or run for the Senate. Bobby Kennedy was urging him to run for the Senate. At the same time, Hughes was urging Kennedy to run for president. Hughes running for the Senate was contingent, in part, on Kennedy agreeing to help him raise money and to obtain an advantageous position in the Senate.

On December 16, 1967, Harold Hughes announced his decision to enter the race for the United States Senate. When asked a question about the war in September 1968, he responded: "The most important and immediate goal must be to bring an end — as soon as possible — to the sacrifice of American lives in a civil war thousands of miles from our homeland …"[23]

He said in October 1968: "I think the basic question we have to face is: Do we end war by making more war … by stubbornly adhering to the same hardline policy we have followed in the past?"[24]

Governor Hughes was elected to the Senate in a very tough race with a small margin of victory. As the new senator from Iowa, he continued his opposition to the Vietnam War. "His views on the war closely paralleled those of the Senate's most outspoken 'doves'."[25]

Notes

1 Kibbie, Jack, Former Iowa State Senator, Emmetsburg, Iowa, October 2017.
2 *The Palimpsest*, The 62nd General Assembly of Iowa, The State Historical Society of Iowa, Iowa City, Iowa, November 1965.
3 Kibbie, Jack, Former Iowa State Senator, Emmetsburg, Iowa, October 2017.
4 Ibid.
5 Ibid.
6 *The Palimpsest*, The 62nd General Assembly of Iowa, The State Historical Society of Iowa, Iowa City, Iowa, November 1967.
7 Gannon, William, Former House of Representatives Minority Leader 1967, Interview, November 2017.
8 *The Palimpsest*, The 62nd General Assembly of Iowa, The State Historical Society of Iowa, Iowa City, Iowa, November 1967.
9 Ibid.
10 Ibid.
11 *Executive Journal*, State of Iowa, State Historical Building, Des Moines, Iowa, 2017.
12 From recordings made by Harold Hughes in anticipation of his writing a book.
13 Hedlund, William, Administrative Assistant to Harold E. Hughes, 1966.
14 Hughes, Harold E., Governor, University of Iowa Library, Special Collections, Amish File, Iowa City, Iowa, 2017.
15 Ibid.
16 Ibid.
17 Ibid.
18 Ibid.
19 Laws of the Sixty-Second General Assembly, Chapter 248, Exemption from Compulsory Education. July 26, 1967, Des Moines, Iowa.
20 Schneider, Dick, *Harold E. Hughes, The Man from Ida Grove*, Chosen Books, Lincoln, Virginia, 1979.
21 Ibid.
22 Ibid.
23 Statement, Hughes, Harold E., KMA Radio, Shenandoah, Iowa, September 1968.
24 Guest Editorial, Hughes, Harold E., KIOA Radio, Des Moines, Iowa, October 1968.
25 Kotz, Nick and Risser, James, "Messiah from the Midwest?," *The Washington Monthly*, May, 1970.

Harold Hughes with longtime friend, Russell Wilson, during a 1979 ceremony at Morningside College in Sioux City, Iowa where Hughes was awarded an Honorary Doctor of Humanities Degree. As governor, Hughes appointed Wilson to the Board of Control, where he worked closely with the Governor on many initiatives, including The Iowa Comprehensive Alcoholism Project. Photo: Personal photo, property of Russell Wilson and used with his permission.

CHAPTER SEVENTEEN

The Iowa Comprehensive Alcoholism Project

The governor said, "You know my thinking about recovery, and I want you to talk to several leaders in the field of alcoholism and addiction. Then I want you to develop a program and prepare a proposal to Sargent Shriver and the War on Poverty." I, somewhat dazed by such a huge challenge asked, "Is there a deadline on this assignment?" The governor said, "Yes, you have one week." One week!

RUSSELL WILSON

In the late spring of 1966, Governor Hughes recognized the need for a rehabilitation program for alcoholics in Iowa. In order to bring the goal to reality, he submitted a request for funds to the Federal Office of Opportunity that was funding programs to combat poverty. Regarding that request, the governor related: "I had been recovered from alcoholism myself for some time prior to entering public life and had worked to try to help many other alcoholics on an individual basis. Becoming governor gave me an opportunity to reach out to help others on a wider scale.

"Iowa already had a Commission on Alcoholism started by a previous governor, but no real program for treatment and rehabilitation. When I became governor, I kept the commission and appointed people like Ray Harrison, a municipal judge from Des Moines, to the Commission. Ray was himself a recovered alcoholic and told me that he had been in his own jail eighteen times — this was before he became a judge. He was then a practicing attorney in Des Moines, and after he was sober a year, wanted to do something to help other men. He [Harrison] called the police station and asked them to give him the number and dates of arrests of 'one of your good drunks,' and the chief said, 'I will give you yours.'"[1]

Hughes continued, "I also decided to apply for a grant from the Office of Economic Opportunity, an agency President Johnson initiated as part of his "Great Society." Johnson had a true concern for the poor. Had it not been for the war in Vietnam, he would have gone down in history as a great president. Johnson had named Sargent Shriver, a brother-in-law to the late President Kennedy, to head The War on Poverty.

"The bureaucrats in Washington were sitting on the OEO application. So I decided to appeal directly to the president. Lyndon Johnson had invited me to give the seconding speech for his nomination during the Democratic Convention that was to be held in Atlantic City. He also invited me to the White House in July of 1964 to talk about the convention and the campaign. I had been assigned to the Lincoln bedroom, but the president invited me down to his room to talk. While the president sat on his bed in his pajamas, I made my pitch for the alcoholism grants. Much to my surprise, the president agreed to do it, and the red tape was promptly removed. We got the grant."[2]

Governor Hughes called Russ Wilson, then a member of the Board of Control of State Institutions, over to his office. Hughes told Wilson that he had been to Washington, D.C. He had talked with President Lyndon Johnson and the head of the War on Poverty, Sargent Shriver, about funding for a program to combat alcoholism. Hughes made a convincing case that alcoholism contributed greatly to the loss of jobs, absenteeism, family dysfunction, and individual and family poverty. He argued that if alcoholics were to be rehabilitated, the result would be increased employment, productivity, and economic stability. The end result would be individuals and families lifted out of poverty, functioning independently, more able to enjoy a normal lifestyle and contribute to society.

The governor said, "You know my thoughts about recovery. I want you to talk to several leaders in the field of alcoholism and addiction. Then I want you to develop a program and prepare a proposal to

Shriver and the War on Poverty." Wilson, somewhat dazed by such a huge challenge asked, "Is there a deadline on this assignment?" The Governor said, "Yes, you have one week." One week!

Wilson recruited two men whom he knew to be quite capable: one was a psychologist and the other an occupational therapist for the State Division of Vocational Rehabilitation. Wilson spent several days interviewing professionals in the field of alcoholism rehabilitation and some individuals who were recovering alcoholics. He recorded their thoughts, observations, experiences, and recommendations regarding a possible program.

Wilson and his two program creators/writers met each afternoon late in the day to discuss various aspects of the proposal and to organize the information into a proposal. Each took one aspect of the proposal and wrote a draft to be critiqued the next afternoon. Before the end of the week, Wilson recruited a professional accountant to develop a budget for the proposed program, which totaled one million dollars.

The following Monday, Wilson flew to Washington and presented the proposal and budget to Sargent Shriver. Shriver was pleased and commented that it was one of the best proposals he had ever received. The proposed request with a million dollar budget was approved.

The proposal created the Iowa Comprehensive Alcoholism Project (ICAP), and Hughes commissioned Wilson to serve as acting director to get the new program organized and to hire the staff of five specialists.

The program recognized that there were very few options in Iowa for the rehabilitation of alcoholics. There were few, if any, facilities that provided transition service and support for recovering alcoholics. Another problem was that although there were some services available to recovering alcoholics, they were spread out in several locations in the populated area. As a result, it was very difficult for anyone, especially a person who was struggling with recovery from alcoholism, to identify, find, and access the services they needed. Those services included, among others, medical care, psychological counseling, employment, job training or retraining, vocational rehabilitation, family counseling, family healthcare, housing, transitional housing, financial counseling, and financial support.

One of the goals of ICAP was to work with the various service providers to facilitate cooperation and coordination between the services to assist recovering alcoholics and their families. The plan called for eight local service centers located in major population areas of the state. Three halfway houses were established to provide temporary housing and support services for recovering alcoholics, especially those being released from jail or prison. The service centers were organized and staffed to function for the life of the grant.

ICAP was organized and funded for several years. A letter written by Judge Bennett of Fort Dodge, Iowa, was found in the Hughes' collection in the University of Iowa Library. An excerpt from the letter attests to the success of the program. "When Lyman Laws first came to Fort Dodge and explained his ICAP program to me, I was most apprehensive. I felt that this would be just another group of social workers that did not understand the program and the needs of the people and that they would pick out only a selected few to help. I advised Mr. Laws of this and also told him that I thought that their biggest problem was going to be to obtain community support.

"Only a few months have passed since ICAP has come into Fort Dodge, and I am pleased and happy to report to you that the local office has won the respect of the authorities and of the people in our community. They have very carefully explained their program and have implemented it to the fullest extent of their ability concerning the limited funds with which they have to operate. Their results have been most remarkable. As a police judge I know of several cases of persons who were nothing more than derelicts and bums who have become sober, industrious, and have been returned to a useful life in their community.

"One of the things that impresses me the most about this program under the leadership of Lyman Laws, is that no one is mollycoddled; they are counseled and are advised as to exactly what help they can receive from ICAP, and they have received that help. Most important also is the fact that ICAP has counseled with and helped people of all economic levels and particularly those without funds and without employment, those people who would otherwise not receive help.

"ICAP and Lyman Laws have progressed extremely well in the few months that they have been here to serve their community and its citizens. I thought that you would be interested in my observations of the program."

Another letter was found in Hughes' papers. In that letter to Governor Hughes in February of 1968, Mr. Patrick W. Antrim, a recovering alcoholic, from Council Bluffs, Iowa, wrote:

"My name is Patrick W. Antrim; I am writing to you in reference to the Iowa Comprehensive Alcoholism Project. I am not sure that you are aware of how much good this program is doing for our community, and I personally wish to inform you of my feelings towards this project.

"The undersigned has been very close and worked with ICAP in this area. We have seen miracles performed before our very eyes in the past several months.

"A college graduate, majoring in accounting, started drinking at an early age and continued drinking into the depth of alcoholism for approximately twelve years. He was hospitalized numerous times in one of our state institutes at a tremendous tax dollar cost. Approximately a year ago this individual was once more released from our state institute; at this time, he was processed through ICAP and referred to me. Since this time, the individual has been rehabilitated, has gotten a job, enrolled in a re-training program at a local trade school, has a place to stay, clothing, and is attending AA meetings and helping to work with others.

"There are five other such cases almost parallel to the foregoing. The cost to ICAP for these six rehabilitation cases is very, very nominal in comparison to the cost of hospital treatment. It also has been reported to me that ICAP is functioning at approximately the same success in other areas of the state. The people of this area are quite confident that ICAP will be the solution to the problem of alcoholism in every state of the union, returning thousands and thousands back to jobs and society as useful citizens. Mr. Hughes you must not let this project fail under any circumstances."

In another letter to Governor Hughes found in Iowa City, dated February 1, 1968, Robert R. Siegrist, director of United Trade Schools, wrote: "When asked by ICAP if we would consider taking some rather hopeless cases into school and see what could be done, I, rather reluctantly, said yes. Quite frankly, government programs don't enthrall me, but when we receive the cooperation from ICAP that we are receiving, it becomes a different story. They are doing a good job. Returning people to good citizenry is wonderful. Saving literally millions in tax dollars isn't bad. I am now on the citizens committee of ICAP and feel that the program must be carried on."

Notes

1 From recordings made by Harold Hughes in anticipation of his writing a book.
2 Ibid.

During his tenure as Governor, Hughes supported legislation that would create Oakdale, a new correctional facility in Iowa City, to provide psychiatric assessment and treatment for mentally ill inmates. Russell Wilson successfully negotiated for a tract of forty acres of land in Iowa City owned by the University of Iowa where the Oakdale facility would be built. This personal photo signed by Hughes to Russ Wilson in 1966 is indicative of the close working and personal relationship they shared.
Photo: Official state photo, from Russell Wilson's personal collection.

CHAPTER EIGHTEEN

Mental Hospitals and Prisons

One day the governor called Russ Wilson over to his office. Hughes told Wilson he wanted him to meet with the president of the University of Iowa and the dean of the College of Medicine to negotiate for a tract of 40 acres of land in Iowa City owned by the University. The goal of the governor was to establish a hospital on that location for the evaluation and treatment of mentally ill inmates. The University's budget was pending in the Iowa Legislature.

RUSSELL WILSON

One of Hughes' many accomplishments as governor was the huge improvements made in Iowa's prisons, mental hospitals, and hospital-schools for the mentally challenged.

On Russ Wilson's first day of work on the Board of Control of State Institutions he reported to the office in the Lucas State Office Building in Des Moines. The Governor invited the members of the board over to his office to welcome Wilson. By the time the board members arrived a few minutes later, the warden at the Anamosa prison was on the phone telling the governor that the inmates were threatening to riot unless the members of the board came to the prison to hear their grievances. At 9:50 am that morning, the state plane lifted off the runway in Des Moines to deliver the board members to the prison.

At the prison, the board met with several groups of very angry, highly agitated, and frustrated prisoners and heard their grievances. Those were very tense but valuable encounters.

Among their complaints was the over-crowded condition in the cellblocks. The inmates were angry about the quality of guards that was determined by the poverty-level salaries the guards were paid. The inmates were concerned about homosexuality, contraband, and prison guard corruption. The men were also angry about the lack of rehabilitation services, education opportunities for inmates, and the absence of psychiatric services for the mentally ill. A major concern was the lack of showers available to inmates who worked in the shops. On a 100-degree day in August, inmates had access to only one shower per week and the cells were not air-conditioned.

Another issue raised was that inmates made little beverage heaters out of clothes hangers and other wire called 'stingers.' With these 'stingers' they could heat a cup of coffee or tea in their cells. Frequently those little "stingers" would blow the fuse in the cellblock, making electrical appliances inoperable.

The Board noted those issues and the fact that the prison budgets provided only $240.00 per month in salary for each prison guard. They also noted the total lack of services for mentally ill inmates. The issue of low salaries for support staff also affected the four mental hospitals and the hospital schools for the mentally challenged.

As a result of those meetings, the Board recommended that the governor strongly support budget provisions to increase salaries, provide rehabilitation services, and to make improvements in the electrical system at the Anamosa prison. They also recommended additional programs and salary increases at the mental hospitals and for the hospital schools for the mentally challenged.

Hughes strongly supported the recommendations and submitted legislation that provided for the creation of a new correctional facility, Oakdale, in Iowa City, for the purpose of providing psychiatric assessment and treatment of mentally ill inmates.

One day the governor called Wilson into this office. Hughes told him he wanted him to meet with the President of the University of Iowa and the Dean of the College of Medicine to negotiate for a tract of forty acres of land in Iowa City owned by the university where the governor's goal was to establish the Oakdale facility. The university's budget was pending in the Iowa Legislature. Wilson met with the two gentlemen at a motel in Grinnell and the University of Iowa officials agreed to relinquish the land for that purpose. The legislature passed the legislation and Oakdale became the first facility in the State of Iowa dedicated to the evaluation and treatment of mentally ill inmates.

Governor Harold Hughes signing a proclamation surrounded by officials and constituents. Photo: *Register and Tribute* commercial photo, State Historical Society of Iowa, Des Moines.

CHAPTER NINETEEN

Crisis Convocations

(Late 1967) Russ Wilson arranged for the governor to meet with the pastors of the Black churches in Des Moines. The governor and Wilson met with the ministers in the basement of a small church a few blocks east of the capitol. After dinner, Hughes got up and began to share his deep concerns. While he was talking, the phone rang and Wilson answered. It was one of Hughes' aids. He said that Martin Luther King had been fatally shot. The governor reluctantly shared the bad news with the group. The room erupted with moans of anguish, pain, and disbelief. The group dispersed into the night.

RUSSELL WILSON

The 1960s and 1970s were years of racial tension. Riots were erupting all over the country. 1967 was a particularly explosive year of racial riots and burning and looting of cities. Des Moines and Waterloo, Iowa were both sites of some of these events. The governor was deeply concerned about these demonstrations. He organized several gatherings around the state known as crisis convocations, where he addressed his concerns.

In 1967, Governor Hughes had what might be called an epiphany, an awakening. Nick Kotz and James Risser described that awakening in their *Washington Monthly* article, 'Messiah from the Midwest?' "The 1967 Harold Hughes, who coped courageously and delicately with Iowa's rural Amish, still seemed strangely insensitive to growing issues of race and poverty. Just as he hesitated at becoming involved in the quickly-maligned war on poverty (Iowa was the forty-ninth state to qualify for participation in the program), Hughes did not push adoption of an open-housing law being considered by the Legislature."

Kotz and Risser continue, "'He's always had some compassion toward the races,' remembers one fellow state official, 'but as late as 1967, he didn't seem to think open housing was a 'must' issue. Some of the Democratic legislators wanted Hughes to push for it, but he just didn't see it. Strangely enough, the basically conservative legislature, goaded by the emotional eloquence of a Black legislator from Cedar Rapids, did see it and passed a new law forbidding discrimination in housing.

"Immediately thereafter, the education of Harold Hughes began on matters of poverty and racism. Without disputing his assertion that he always wanted to help 'the underprivileged and forgotten,' it is clear that few other Iowans, including Hughes, had bothered to focus on the problems of Iowa's one percent Black population, isolated in a few urban enclaves. As for poverty, it is finely masked behind the deceptive veneer of rich, rolling cornfields and Iowa-proud self-sufficiency. Hughes simply had not seen or felt the problem and could not identify with it. Obviously, he should have read about a Black revolution raging across the country, but Hughes's concerns were strictly Iowan then and his commitment on issues does not come from books.

"As minor episodes of racial violence struck Des Moines and Waterloo in the summer of 1967, Hughes suddenly and secretly visited the economically-depressed ghetto areas of Iowa's cities. Just as four years earlier he had immersed himself in problems of men behind state penitentiary walls, now he went through the invisible walls of much larger prisons.

"'I was humbled and I was ashamed by suddenly realizing my own ignorance,' he soon publicly admitted. 'For a lifetime I have lived in this state and never believed that these conditions exist. And, frankly, I have to confess that if I had cared enough, I would have looked. I found that I didn't know my state, as I should. I was physically and spiritually ill. People had poured out to me their bitterness and their loss of hope. Reassessing morally my own position, I found myself bearing the guilt.'"[1]

In late December of 1967, as a result of his awakening to the poverty, racism, and loss of hope in Iowa, Governor Hughes shared with Russ Wilson his concerns. At the time, Wilson was serving in the office of Bishop James Thomas, the Methodist Bishop of Iowa. Those concerns included the Black revolution raging across the country, racial riots in the south, burning and looting in many cities, and rising tensions over unemployment, poverty, and inequality among Blacks and unrest in the ghettos of Iowa. The two considered what could be done and agreed that the churches, including the bishops, rabbis, and denominational executives needed to be involved. The issues were spiritual as well as social, economic, and political.

Governor Hughes decided to meet with the Methodist Bishop, James Thomas, who was an African American, to discuss the possible involvement of the churches. He also wanted to meet with the pastors of the Black churches in Des Moines to share with them his concerns about the 'racial crises.' Hughes wanted to meet with Bishop Thomas privately without publicity. That meeting was arranged. The two and Wilson met at Wilson's home for lunch.

Hughes shared his concern for the unrest in the state, the racial tensions, and what he considered to be a 'crisis.' The decision was made to ask the bishops, rabbis, and denominational leaders of the state to sponsor and organize several public meetings in Iowa. Those meetings would provide a platform for Governor Hughes to address the issues and share his concerns with the people of Iowa.

In the meantime, Wilson arranged for the governor to meet with the pastors of the Black churches in Des Moines. The governor and Wilson met with the ministers in the basement of a small church a few blocks east of the capitol. After dinner, Hughes got up and began to share his deep concerns. While he was talking the phone rang and Wilson answered. It was one of Hughes' aides. He said that Martin Luther King had been fatally shot. The governor reluctantly shared the bad news with the group. The room erupted with moans of anguish, pain, and disbelief. The group dispersed into the night.

Plans were made to hold 'Convocations on Crisis' meetings in six cities sponsored by the state's religious leaders: Council Bluffs,

Davenport, Waterloo, Sioux City, Cedar Rapids, and Des Moines. The religious leaders flew to each location in a caravan of planes. Three thousand people attended the meeting at North High School in Des Moines. Attendance in the other cities was equally high. Hughes was powerful. His deep voice conveyed his concerns about the issues and the need for decisive action.

The so called 'crisis convocations' were considered to be 'a unique ecumenical' church-state position. They were planning to inform every citizen of the crisis that existed. They were also planning to arouse all citizens to take action to solve the problems before they got worse.

"The awakened governor responded quickly, persuading key business leaders in several of the cities to set up emergency employment programs for ghetto youth." He followed through in the fall by meeting with Iowa religious leaders, then summoned lay and religions leaders in six principle cities to 'Convocations on Crisis.' "Hughes' personal and emotional confession stirred his listeners and led to the creation of civic task forces and new privately-financed employment programs. Jobs were provided for 1,200 youths in the summer of 1968. It was a fascinating example of Hughes' persuasive powers, which, on a person-to-person level, have a mesmerizing quality.

"Watching him eloquently and powerfully lecture those businessmen about racism, one could sense that the 1958 'porpoise in the fishbowl' had burst free. The original, elemental qualities still produced the commanding leadership, but they now were refined, broadened, and under firm, confident self-control. Once Hughes feels a problem, as one observer puts it, he exhibits 'a combination of political pragmatism and social conscience' in finding solutions.

"The social conscience flows out of deep religious feelings — from a lifelong Methodist who says, 'Religion has been the motivating force in my life.' It helped him quit drinking and to decide 'that if God has a purpose for me I would try to follow it. I had messed up my life. Religion has taught me to love people, to be patient when I'm an impatient man, to respect the views of others whom I disagree with, to do good to others where harm has been intended to me.'"[2]

Note: The complete address that Hughes delivered at the crisis convocations is available in the Harold Hughes papers in the library at the University of Iowa.

Notes

1 Kotz, Nick and Risser, James, "Messiah from the Midwest?," *The Washington Monthly*, May, 1970.

2 Ibid.

Iowa state executives elected in 1964.
(Left to right) State Treasurer Paul Franzenburg, Attorney General Larry Scalise, Lieutenant Governor Robert Fulton, Governor Hughes, Secretary of State Gary Cameron, State Auditor Lorne Worthington, and Secretary of Agriculture Ken Owens. Photo: Official state photo.

CHAPTER TWENTY

Philosophy and Practice of Government

I contrive it to be my responsibility to stand for the things that are right for Iowa, regardless of the consequences.

HAROLD E. HUGHES

Harold Hughes was a very powerful and effective politician, governor, and U.S. Senator. One might ask why he was so effective. The authors believe Hughes' actions as an individual, a governor, and a U.S. senator as well as his political philosophy and practice of government, all played a role in his success.

One principal or conviction that is obvious from his run for the Commerce Commission through his tenure as a U.S. senator is his identification with, and commitment to, the plight of the "little man," the underdog, the powerless in society. That quality was evident again and again beginning with his awareness of the deceitful, if not illegal, policies and practices of the Iowa State Commerce Commission. The commission, influenced by generous gifts and favors from, in Hughes' words, 'the goddamn big truckers,' favored and entitled the big companies to the disadvantage of small, individual truckers like himself. That conviction actually helped to catapult Hughes into politics.

Recognition of and concern for the underdog was evident when he visited the state penitentiaries and personally met with every inmate who was on death row and commuted the sentence for several which he did not believe deserved such harsh penalties.

His concern for the marginalized was obvious when, as governor, Hughes pushed for and successfully influenced the legislature to substantially increase the budgets of the prisons and mental hospitals of the state. His concern for mentally ill inmates in the state prisons resulted in the creation of the Oakdale facility for the evaluation and treatment of mentally ill inmates.

When he went to the predominately Black enclaves of Waterloo and Des Moines and met one-on-one with the poor, hopeless, and marginalized people there, his compassion for the disadvantaged was evident.

As governor, Hughes was personally involved with his constituents and with the pertinent issues of the day. Stories abound of Hughes personally spending time with alcoholics who reached out for help, including some U.S. senators.

Hughes was forthright, transparent, honest, and direct in expressing his thoughts and beliefs in dealing with relevant issues. Those qualities were evident when he confronted the sensitive issue of liquor by the drink. It shows in his dealing with the Vietnam War and with his compassion and actions after visiting the ghettos of Des Moines and Waterloo. His transparency and honesty were evident when he confessed that he had failed to inform himself with the plight of the people in those enclaves.

Another of Hughes' principles about government is that it should concern itself with justice. Again, early in his career as an individual truck driver, and later as the operator of the Iowa Better Trucking Bureau, he felt the Commerce Commission was dealing with small truckers unjustly. They were favoring the large commercial operators at the expense of the small, independent operators.

One could debate whether vision fits into the "philosophy of government" but it is not debatable whether or not Harold Hughes possessed vision. What we refer to as 'vision' may be Hughes' ability to see what needed to be done and his gift of articulating that need. In the long list of legislation that was introduced and passed on his watch as governor, his ability to see the need and to take action are clear.

"In 1962, he [Hughes] defeated incumbent Republican Governor Norman Erbe and commenced the first of his three successive two-year terms in the gold-domed Iowa Statehouse. On the surface it seemed ironic that reformed drunk Hughes had been elected by speaking boldly in favor of legalized liquor-by-the-drink in Bible belt, dry, conservative Iowa. In reality, he was igniting a revolution in Iowa politics. The state was in the throes of transition from a rural to an urban economy and urban mores and was without any political leadership.

"...As he would on many future issues, Hughes tapped a latent majority who desired a more progressive state image (they never tired of jokes about the little old lady from Dubuque and about key clubs) and who wanted more of their political leaders than cautious mediocracy."[1]

In a speech to 15,000 people in Madison Square Garden in March 1972 Hughes declared, "We are here to bury the false and shoddy propaganda that the peace movement in America is dead." He called for a total restructuring of national policies "to break cleanly and drastically with the past ... not the superficial change, but major surgery."[2]

Again, this quality may not be considered a 'philosophy of government.' Rather than avoiding or delaying dealing with very difficult and politically sensitive issues, Hughes' custom was to face them with courage and determination. That quality is evident in his action on the Iowa State Commerce Commission. It was demonstrated when he became involved in the Amish School issue. Perhaps it is most evident when Hughes, a former hawk and supporter of the Vietnam War, strongly and publicly opposed the war and the powerful president, Lyndon Johnson.

"Toward the end of 1963, Hughes went into his familiar shell, annoyed by detached decision-making and perplexed about a legislature-approved reapportionment plan that was going to the voters. Most Democratic political leaders advised him not to oppose the plan, which supposedly was popular with rural and small-town voters who would be given ironclad minority control of one legislative chamber. Finally, with a click into sharp focus on the issue, Hughes plunged into the struggle and, against long odds, defeated the plan almost single-handedly. The plan was unfair, and Hughes said so flatly, though there was not yet a one-man, one-vote decree to back him up."[3]

Another principle that guided Hughes in governing was obvious in his involvement in the Amish School controversy. Later Hughes said, "I always recognized the logic and the integrity of those who sincerely believed that such an exception [the Amish schools issue] should not be made," he told the Legislature after the bill was approved. "But sometimes it is wiser to be tolerant of non-uniformity and bad laws rather than people."[4]

Another facet of Hughes' philosophy was that it was important to him for a public official to grow in the office. He also believed that it was important for a political party to grow morally as it grows in effectiveness. Hughes also believed that one of the goals of government is to seek a better life for all of its people.

In an article about the governor, Kotz and Risser make this observation about another of Hughes' qualities. "Once Hughes feels a problem, as one observer puts it, he exhibits a combination of political pragmatism and social conscience in finding solutions."

When a U.S. Senate seat would soon be vacated, and Hughes was encouraged by many to run for the seat, he was personally encouraged by then Senator Robert F. Kennedy to run. Hughes, who had been undecided, was persuaded by Kennedy that one man could make a difference in the Senate. Of Kennedy, Hughes said, "The importance he placed on the elements of humanity, peace, and the value of the individual all affected me."[5] Those qualities and philosophies on moral issues resonated with Hughes.

In an article on Hughes in the *Des Moines Register* dated November 3, 1996, James Flansburg wrote: "His faith in his God was equaled and matched by his faith in the people, the voters. He did not believe that a politician had to talk down to his listeners. I am trying to explain the man who — substantially more than anyone else — remade or recast the American political system and, before that, Iowa and local government.

"I'd like to hear from historians weighing in, but I see Hughes as Iowa's most effective governor. The only others to rank with him are Samuel Kirkwood and A. B. Cummins."[6]

To further understand the senator's thoughts about the function of government, following are a few of his related quotations as published in *Iowa, a Biennial History.*[7]

"The most important quality of a public official, as I see it, is the capacity to grow in office. And the most important quality of a political party is to grow in moral stature as its membership and influence increase." *Des Moines Register*, January 18, 1964

"Isn't the goal we are really seeking in Iowa better living for all her people? We want the finest of farms and the best of industries, yes, but above all, we want the good life for our people, both rural and urban, and communities of good homes, churches and schools." Osceola, February 26, 1963

"It is high time we set aside old prejudices, clichés, and special interests that have narrowed our views in the past. It is high time that we moved toward the future of abundance and well-being that lies before all of us if we are willing to work together." Des Moines, February 14, 1963.

"While our party talks of the needs of Iowa for the 1960's and the 1970's, the other party talks in terms of the past, hoping that the pressing problems of today will somehow evaporate and that the good days will return." Tama, August 10, 1963

"We must convince our young people that we are going to expand our state's economy, that we are going to modernize its laws and its governmental structure, that we are going to modernize our tax system and that we will offer them opportunities in education and employment in the years ahead." Sioux City, September 27, 1963

"Some political advisors have recommended that I should keep quiet on this controversial issue. But this is not my nature. It is not the way I was elected to the governorship. It is not the kind of governor I want to be."[8] Sac County Democratic Dinner, September 2, 1963

In late 1967, Governor Hughes had to decide whether to run for a seat in the U.S. Senate or not.

Notes

1 Kotz, Nick, and Risser, James, "Messiah from the Midwest?," *The Washington Monthly*, May, 1970.
2 Ibid.
3 Ibid.
4 Ibid.
5 Flansburg, James, *Des Moines Register*, November 13, 1996.
6 Ibid
7 Wall, Joseph Frazier, *Iowa, A Biennial History*, W. W. Norton & Co., Inc., New York.
8 Ibid.

Senator Hughes' early senate staff stayed with him in his new family home in McLean, Virginia, while his wife, Eva, and daughter, Phyllis, stayed in Des Moines so Phyllis could finish her school term. (From left to right) Senator Hughes, Bill Hedlund (author), a member of Hughes' staff from 1964 – 1972, Ed Campbell, and Park Rinard.
Photo: Personal photo used with permission from the Hughes family.

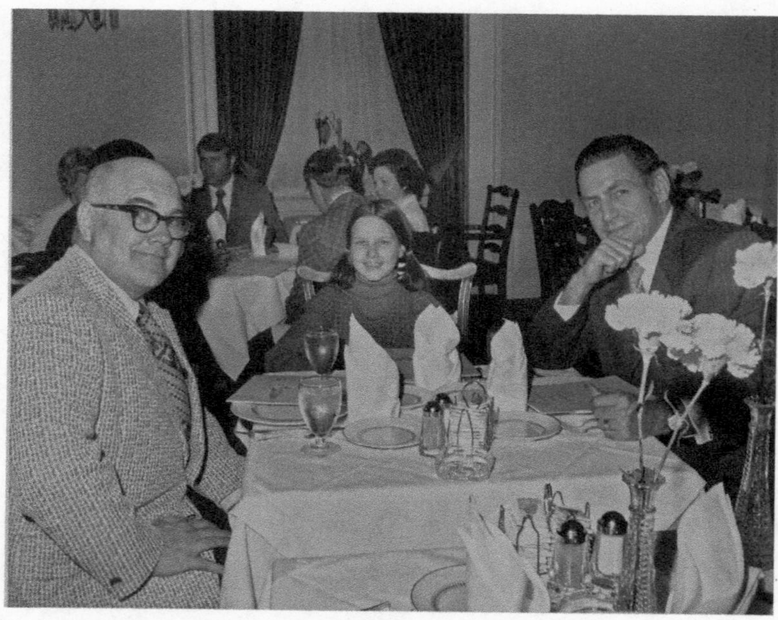

The author, Russ Wilson and his daughter, Kristin, with Hughes in the Senate Dining Room in Washington, D.C., 1973. Photo: Personal family photo used with permission of Russ Wilson.

CHAPTER TWENTY-ONE

Running for the Senate

Many people had talked with Hughes urging him to run for the Senate. He did not want to live in Washington, D.C. … Robert Kennedy made him feel "that I owed it not only to myself, but to America, God, and everything else."[1]

JOURNAL INTERVIEW 39, *ADDICTION*

Governor Hughes spoke to the Greater Baltimore Area Council on Alcoholism in Baltimore in late 1967. A press conference followed. The question was asked if he was going to run for reelection as governor or run for the Senate. Hughes said "he was tired and no governor had been in office for more than three terms (at that time a term was two years). He had no interest in running for the Senate. There were opportunities for jobs in the private sector, but he was keeping his options open. He probably wouldn't run again. After the press conference, a reporter said to him privately that he had to run for the Senate, "as your state and the country need you there." Hughes stated he was not qualified and didn't have the ability to be a U.S. senator. The reporter told him 'You're dead wrong.'"[2]

A week later Robert Kennedy called Hughes and said the reporter, a friend of both of them, had called Kennedy to tell of this conversation and that Hughes was not running for governor or the Senate. Kennedy told Hughes his voice and vote were needed in the Senate to end the Vietnam War. Also, Kennedy pledged he would help Hughes do the things he would like to do on alcoholism. Kennedy invited Hughes to come to New York so they could talk about it. "Hughes told Kennedy that he should consider running for president. Kennedy said that wasn't what the discussion was to be about. Hughes said that maybe it should be. You want me to run for the Senate, and we have to have someone run against Johnson for President."[3]

Hughes went to New York. He and Kennedy talked in the afternoon prior to the Empire State Dinner. Many people had talked with Hughes, urging him to run for the Senate. He did not want to live in Washington D.C. He did not like the obligation of a six-year term. Robert Kennedy made him feel "that I owed it not only to myself, but to America, God, and everything else … that whatever my voice could be in the area I wanted to serve so badly, which was alcoholism, I should do it. I had never thought of it that way before."[4]

Governor Hughes' own personal story of alcoholism and the establishment of a state program in Iowa led to his interest at the federal level. He asked Bobby Kennedy if he could be involved and be an influence at the federal level of government. Kennedy said if Hughes were elected, he would help him obtain an appointment to an appropriate committee. His brother, Ted Kennedy, was chairman of the Health Subcommittee of the Labor and Public Welfare in the Senate. They would work something out. A very important consideration of running was money. Hughes had no money, so he asked Kennedy if he was willing to help raise funds. Kennedy said he would commit to raising funds. Hughes had a date he wanted for a fundraiser. Kennedy said he would do it if the governor would run for the Senate. Kennedy said, "I commit myself to you, Governor, one thousand percent. You need to run for the Senate. You may make the difference."[5] Hughes said he was going home to talk with his family and some friends and would call Kennedy in a few days.

Hughes talked with his family about running. They agreed he should run. The other person he talked with was Park Rinard, his friend and mentor who had been with him since he first ran for the Iowa State Commerce Commission, who agreed to go to Washington with him.

Hughes called Robert Kennedy and told him he would run. Kennedy said he would come to Iowa and support him. Hughes announced he would enter the race for the United States Senate.

Don't Mess with Grandma Lillian

When Hughes was in the senate, his wife, Eva's mother, Lillian Schoor, and his daughter, Carol, lived with them for a while. Carol's second marriage had been to a fellow who, in his daughter, Phyllis' words "turned out to be a creep." They had been divorced for some time.

On one occasion Carol and Grandmother Lillian were having lunch in a local restaurant when the ex-creep appeared and sat down in the booth next to Carol. He proceeded to take hold of Carol's arm with a strong and unwanted grip. Carol asked him to let go. When he refused, Grandma Lillian took a steak knife, reached across the table, pressed the knife against his throat and said, "If you don't let go of her, I'll cut your throat."

The creep let go and left the restaurant.[6]

Notes

1 "Conversation with Senator Harold Hughes," Journal Interview 39, *Addiction*, Washington D.C., 1997.
2 Ibid.
3 Ibid.
4 Ibid.
5 Ibid.
6 From recordings made by Harold Hughes in anticipation of his writing a book.

During his tenure as senator, Harold Hughes continued his personal mission of addressing alcoholism and addiction, here in a speech at the Edgehill Newport Foundation in Virginia. Personal family photo used with permission of the Hughes family.

CHAPTER TWENTY-TWO

Accomplishments in the Senate

During the debate Senator Jacob Javits of New York paid tribute to Senator Hughes. Senator Javits and Senator Moss had worked for years to get Congress to tackle the issue. 'Javits said the proposal had no action until Hughes provided his very gifted leadership as a result of his unique and long-standing commitment to the solution of the problem.' [1]

JAMES RISSER

When Hughes was elected to the U.S. Senate in 1968 he wasted no time getting to work on one of his personal missions, addressing alcoholism. Upon his election, he chose to become a member of the Labor and Public Welfare Committee. Senator Ralph Yarborough of Texas, chairman of the committee, knew Hughes was a recovering alcoholic and was especially interested in the subject of alcoholism. Senator Yarborough created a Special Subcommittee on Alcoholism and Narcotics and took the unusual step of appointing a freshman senator, Harold Hughes, as chairman of the Subcommittee.

For several years Senator Jacob Javits of New York and Senator Frank Moss of Utah had tried to get Congress to address the problems of alcoholism with proposed legislation for the treatment of the disease. However, their efforts had not been successful.

Senator Hughes announced that the subcommittee would hold three days of hearings from July 23–25, 1969, to examine the impact of alcoholism and narcotics. In his opening statement the first day of the hearings, Hughes said, "This is a new kind of subcommittee and the first devoted to the cause of helping individual citizens and society gain relief from the human blights of drug and alcohol abuse."[2] He emphasized that the subcommittee's approach would focus on health rather than law enforcement and aimed to provide general information. That was a huge change in the approach to alcoholism and drug addiction. The main objectives of the subcommittee as viewed by Hughes were: "1) to dramatize to Congress and the public the magnitude and urgency of these problems, 2) to develop new approaches to helping people in our society who are afflicted by alcoholism and drug abuse, and 3) to develop legislation that is practical and on a realistic financial scale not previously dreamed of by this government."[3]

In the hearings, Judge Ray Harrison, Municipal Court Judge, Des Moines, Iowa, and a recovering alcoholic, "told of the many cases that came before him in which alcohol was the basic problem. Every Wednesday night, Judge Harrison held an Alcoholics Anonymous-like meeting in his courtroom for individuals with drinking problems. He reported that the first night two people attended, but attendance had grown to around 200."[4]

"Reverend David Works, an Episcopal clergyman, a recovering alcoholic, and a member of Alcoholics Anonymous, was chief executive officer of the North Conway Institute. Reverend Works said his interdenominational organization concentrated on the prevention of problem drinking and other forms of drug dependency, as well as the treatment and rehabilitation of persons in trouble with alcohol and other chemicals."[5]

"Reverend Lewis Sheen told the committee how he was able to hide his alcoholism for years. Eventually, he drank more and more and found it harder to wait until late in the day to start drinking. The effect on his wife and two sons was dramatic. Finally, after a very bad episode, a friend helped him check into a hospital for six weeks. He said, 'Here I sit before you a man of fifty years of age and no job. I am going to have to begin all over again at fifty and make a new life for my family and myself. Money is scarce … but I hope to find a life working with brother alcoholics and their families.'"[6]

Miss Mercedes McCambridge, Academy Award-winning actress and a recovering alcoholic, said "she was convinced that her disease can be arrested. She pointed out that social life is very caught up in drinking. When you go to someone's home or a restaurant, the

'Welcome' is frequently followed by 'What would you like to drink?' The chemicals in alcohol put people at ease. The alcoholic himself must break the chain of self-destruction by admitting, recognizing, and accepting the disease."[7]

"Bill W., co-founder of Alcoholics Anonymous (AA), told the subcommittee that his doctor informed his wife that he could not help keep Bill sober, as he was a victim of a compulsion to drink, in spite of his strong desire to stay sober. After a stay in the hospital for depression, Bill said he 'eventually had a very sudden spiritual awakening in which I was released from the compulsion to drink, a compulsion on my mind morning, noon, and night for several years.' After this, he decided to help other alcoholics coming out of hospitals. Eventually, Bill and a doctor founded Alcoholics Anonymous. Bill said, 'The virtues of AA are not really earned virtues. It is a matter of do or die. Nothing is too good for the next sufferer. Our dedication is first based on the fact that our lives and fortunes have been saved and we want to share this with the next fellow, knowing that it is a part of the maintenance of our own recovery and life or death. So, this is the source of the great dedication that you see among AA.'"[8]

"Thomas Pike, vice chairman of a corporate board and a recovering alcoholic, started a program to help alcoholics in his own company. He said that generally the corporate structure from top to bottom believes alcoholism only occurs in the skid-row element. However, that is only three to five percent of the alcoholic population. This means that over ninety percent of alcoholics are people employed in industries, professions, and government."[9]

The subcommittee learned about treatment services for alcoholics from a panel of individuals working in hospitals, mental health facilities, and the Institute for Justice. A person from the Department of Social Services and a state director of alcoholism treatment from the Veterans' Administration also testified. They all told of problems they encountered and successes in the treatment of alcoholics. Several other panelists testified on the final day of the hearings on alcoholism in Washington D.C.[10]

Hearings were also held in New York City, Los Angeles, and Denver. The testimony in all of the cities conveyed the same type of stories heard in Washington. At one of the last hearings one senator complained that he was tired of hearing the same thing over and over again. These hearings showed that alcoholism is no respecter of persons or areas or cities. People with alcohol problems come from all walks of life. Alcoholism is a health problem and more pervasive than many believe.

Following the hearings, the subcommittee worked to develop a bill to meet the needs of the problem of alcoholism they had learned about in the cities they visited. A bill was reported out to the full Committee on Labor and Public Welfare. The committee approved the bill and reported it out to be placed on the Senate calendar. The proposed legislation was co-sponsored by fifty-two senators.

"Hughes became worried that the schedule and the delays in the Senate might result in the bill dying. He felt the momentum from the bill was now. He persuaded the Senate leadership to interrupt the debate on ABM missile and military procurement long enough to take up the alcoholism bill. It was passed on a unanimous vote. During the debate Senator Jacob Javits of New York paid tribute to Senator Hughes. Senator Javits and Senator Moss had worked for years to get Congress to tackle the issue. 'Javits said the proposal had no action until Hughes provided his very gifted leadership as a result of his unique and long-standing commitment to the solution of the problem.'"[11]

"The legislation authorized grants totaling $300 million over three years to state and local agencies, both public and private, to finance specific projects. Grants of seventy-five million were given to states to assist them in planning and carrying out alcoholism prevention and rehabilitation programs. The attack on alcoholism would be directed at the federal level by a National Institute for the Prevention and Control of Alcohol Abuse and Alcoholism."[12]

This was the first time Congress passed an alcoholism program and funded it. Senator Hughes continued the efforts that he had made as governor and pushed for federal legislation that was successfully passed. It was a major accomplishment for a first term senator.

Senator Hughes also supported legislation in agriculture, rural area development, and conservation. He organized the Midwest Democratic Conference of Senators, a group of fifteen senators from nine farm states that proved to be an effective farm block.

"Hughes was appointed chairman of a newly created subcommittee of the Armed Services Committee on Drug Abuse in the Military. He was intensively involved in the implementation and oversight of the president's counter-offensive against drug abuse in both civilian and military sectors."[13]

Senator Harold Hughes, Senator Mark Hatfield of Oregon, and Senator Harrison Williams of New Jersey introduced legislation to create a temporary Vietnam childcare agency to aid abandoned children in South Vietnam, particularly those fathered by American servicemen. In response to a letter in support of the legislation, Hughes wrote, "It is our hope the legislation creating the temporary Children's Agency will be able to work with the South Vietnamese government to make more feasible laws for the adoption of these children by American citizens … We feel that it is important that the United States must take some responsibility in this problem" of abandoned children fathered by American servicemen.[14]

Senator Hughes worked as a member of the Armed Services Committee in uncovering the secret, unauthorized bombing on North Vietnam and the covert and illegal air war waged in Cambodia in 1969 and 1970. He succeeded in obtaining the disclosure of classified information relating to air raids. In a report to the Senate, Hughes said "there were 3,630 B-52 sorties which dropped 104,000 tons of bombs in the fourteen months prior to May 1970."[15]

The senator made the two following statements that are as relevant today as they were fifty years ago.

Saving Our Environment

"If we are to save our environment and retain a livable world, the old concepts of unlimited creature comforts for every individual citizen, of uninhibited corporate profits, and of politics as usual must be drastically revised. Realistically, what we are talking about is a revolution of values and attitudes. It is not the technology of restoration or method of abatement that is the central concern. … These can be provided. When all of the polite phrases have been spoken and the neat neuter plans have been unveiled, it is our commitment that will tell the story. And when I say commitment, I mean moral and financial commitment. It is a matter of priorities. The supersonic transport can wait. The environment won't." Remarks by Hughes before Southern University's Student Government Association, Memphis, Tennessee, April 25, 1970[16]

"We have a job to do — an incredibly massive job of rebuilding. It is not just a matter of tearing down decaying buildings and erecting new ones. It is a complex matter of rebuilding the basic structures of our society along the lines it was originally intended to have. It can only be accomplished by a majority of our citizens of all races and colors working together relentlessly. The eye of the hurricane is the racial issue, although it must be recognized that this is just one aspect of the overall crisis. From a practical standpoint, the race relations problem is the logical focus of our attention. If we finally face up to this part of our problem, it will mean that we are facing up to the entire problem of the disadvantaged and disinherited in our society." Speech by Senator Hughes to U.S. Senate, March 18, 1970[17]

Notes

1 Riser, James, "Reveal Hughes Helped Senator Kick Alcoholism," *Des Moines Register*, August 11, 1970.

2 The Impact of Alcoholism, Hearings Before the Special Subcommittee on Alcoholism and Narcotics, Ninety First Congress, Washington D.C., 1969.

3 Ibid.

4 Ibid.

5 Ibid.
6 Ibid.
7 Ibid.
8 Ibid.
9 Ibid.
10 Ibid.
11 Riser, James, "Reveal Hughes Helped Senator Kick Alcoholism," *Des Moines Register*, August 11, 1970.
12 Ibid.
13 Senator Harold E. Hughes, A Report to Iowa, *The Senate Years, United States Senate, Washington*, D.C., 1975.
14 Hughes, Harold E., University of Iowa Library Special Collections Division, Iowa City, Iowa, 2017.
15 Senator Harold E. Hughes, *A Report to Iowa, The Senate Years, United States Senate, Washington*, D.C., 1975.
16 The Hughes Committee, 41 Ivy Street S.E., Washington, D.C., 20003.
17 Ibid.

Governor Hughes signing a new tax bill, July 20, 1967.
Photo: State Historical Society of Iowa, Des Moines

CHAPTER TWENTY-THREE

Alcoholism – Out of the Closet

"Harold Hughes devoted his life to the victims of alcoholism and drug addiction. He, more than any other person, was responsible for bringing alcoholism and drug addiction out of the closet of secrecy. He was also for sponsoring and shepherding legislation that offered treatment and many services for alcoholics, addicts, and their families."[1]

DICK SCHROEDER AND HAROLD E. HUGHES
THE MAN FROM IDA GROVE

Phyllis Hughes Ewing reminded us that when her father ran for the Iowa State Commerce Commission and later for governor, that alcoholism was kept tightly in the closet. Phyllis said, "You did not talk about it. You did not admit it, and the family did their best to keep the 'elephant in the room' a secret."

However, the governor blew the doors off of that thinking. When one of his gubernatorial opponents publicly accused him of being an alcoholic, Hughes, on television, admitted that he was an alcoholic who had not taken a drink for five years. Many times after that admission he frankly admitted that he had a history of alcoholism and was in recovery. That was a huge step toward recognizing alcoholism as a treatable disease and a major health issue.

While governor, Hughes initiated the Iowa Comprehensive Alcoholism Project, the mission of which was to assist alcoholics in obtaining sobriety treatment, support, jobs, health care, and other services.

As a U.S. Senator, Hughes had persuaded the Chairman of the Senate's Labor and Public Welfare Committee to establish a Special

Sub Committee on Alcoholism and Narcotics, chaired by Hughes himself. This subcommittee, which gave unprecedented attention to the subject, held public hearings on July 23–25, 1969. A number of people in recovery testified, including Academy Award-winning actress Mercedes McCambridge, National Council on Alcoholism founder Marty Mann, and AA co-founder Bill W. In *The Man from Ida Grove*, Hughes wrote that he asked a dozen other well-known people in recovery to present public testimony, but all declined. The hearings were considered a threat to anonymity and sobriety.

"As senator, Hughes also talked about the need for treatment of drug addiction. He stated that 'treatment is virtually nonexistent because addiction is not recognized as an illness.'"[2] Unfortunately, the hearings and subsequent events related to alcoholism and addiction, were not given much press attention because the press was more interested in the Vietnam War, poverty, and other critical issues. Legislation creating the National Institute on Drug Abuse was not passed until 1974.[3]

"In a time of rapid change for the field, we seldom take time to reflect on its history. We assume that our national and state governments have a degree of interest in prevention and treatment, as a matter of public policy, and that this interest needs only to be strengthened and given a higher profile. We seldom think of a time when there was no such policy, when there was no reference to substance abuse on the public agenda.

"Harold Hughes' most frequently cited achievement was the passage of the Comprehensive Alcohol Abuse and Alcoholism Prevention, Treatment and Rehabilitation Act of 1970, (P.L. 91-616), which came to be known as "The Hughes Act." That legislation established the National Institute on Alcohol Abuse and Alcoholism (NIAAA) and, for the first time, made formula grants available to the states for the development of community-based programs.

"Also included in the Hughes Act were requirements for state planning, incentives for hospitals to admit alcoholics, and confidentiality of patient records. Before 1970, the only federal commitment was a mere four million dollars for treatment grants, and even that was in jeopardy as a result of Nixon Administration cost cutting. Drunk driving had gotten some attention, but hardly in the context of a comprehensive view of the effects of alcohol on society.

"To be sure, the fellowship of Alcoholics Anonymous had already brought help and hope to alcoholics for more than two decades, but it took a Harold Hughes to make alcohol abuse and dependence public issues to beyond the program of attraction, of personal recovery, and make alcohol abuse and dependence matters of public health, welfare and safety.

"Noteworthy as that may be in the history of our field, even more remarkable was how a freshman senator, a man with origins in a small town in Iowa, with only one year of college education and with a personal history of alcoholism that drove him to the point of suicide, came to sponsor the landmark legislation."[4]

"The goal of the 1970 Comprehensive Act, considered a "major milestone" in the nation's efforts to deal with alcohol abuse and alcoholism, was "to help millions of alcoholics recover and to save thousands of lives on highways, reduce crime, decrease the welfare rates, and cut down the appalling economic waste from alcoholism."[5]

"Harold Hughes devoted his life to the victims of alcoholism and drug addiction. He, more than any other person, was responsible for bringing alcoholism and drug addiction out of the closet of secrecy. He was also for sponsoring and shepherding legislation that offered treatment and many services for alcoholics, addicts, and their families."[6]

According to Dick Shroeder in *The Man From Ida Grove*, "The death of Harold Everett Hughes marks the passing of one of the true pioneers in the field of alcohol and other drug abuse. All who work in the field owe a debt of gratitude to Harold Hughes — both for his accomplishments and for his example. More than just a public figure, he has been described by friends and colleagues as a "life force." He was an extraordinary man with an extraordinary career.[7]

Notes

1 Hughes, Harold, with Schroeder, Dick, *The Man from Ida Grove*, Chosen Books, Lincoln, VA.
2 *In Memoriam, Remembering Harold E. Hughes*, www.well.com/user/woa/harolde.htm, Adopted from an obituary by Gerrit DenHartog published in the *"A" Team*, Missouri Division of Alcohol and Drug Abuse.
3 Ibid.
4 Hughes, Harold, with Schroeder, Dick, *The Man from Ida Grove*, Chosen Books, Lincoln, VA.
5 Ibid.
6 Ibid.
7 Hughes, Harold, with Schroeder, Dick, *The Man from Ida Grove*, Chosen Books, Lincoln, VA.

Harold Hughes' boldness and willingness to go where many others would not and meet with people who could talk with him about real problems, was a guiding principle in his political life. He was not afraid to have hard conversations in an effort to find solutions.
Photo: Senator Harold E. Hughes, 1967, State Historical Society of Iowa, Des Moines

CHAPTER TWENTY-FOUR

The Senator Visits A 'Shooting Gallery'

Martha took us across the street to begin our journey into the rubble of the underground to reach the 'shooting gallery.' We went down into the basement of the old tenant buildings and it was difficult to see through the dark, musty, and rubble foundation. The group, Davis, Hughes, Sen. Javits, and the local NBC group, had to crawl on their hands and knees. It was slow going and claustrophobic.[1]

BOB KHOLOS

Sometime during the late 1960s, in the process of researching alcoholism and drug addiction, the senator went to Harlem to visit a 'shooting gallery,' a clandestine location where drug addicts went to practice their addiction. It is doubtful whether any senator before or since has had that experience.

"The tour was arranged by Martha Davis, a dedicated community worker who was working with children and young adults who were addicted to heroin. She wanted the politicians to be exposed to the sobering and tragic environment of addiction.

"As Hughes and others watched, Davis sent a nine-year-old girl from her office on the second floor to buy drugs from a pusher on the street. The child walked up to a fellow, handed him the money and returned with a bag of drugs.

"After that humbling experience, Martha took us across the street to begin our journey into the rubble of the underground to reach the 'shooting gallery.'[2]

Bob Kholos, a journalist now deceased, who accompanied Hughes, described the visit, "...we walked through ankle deep garbage piled around the side of a large housing project." Bob continued, "Men were wearing expensive three-piece suits, members of Hughes' subcommittee, chaperoned by a large Black community worker and a small rag-tag group of press were ready to trip through the dark, underground foundation of an old tenement building in order to reach the heroin shooting gallery.

"We went down into the basement of the old tenement building and it was difficult to see through the dark, musty, and rubble foundation.

"The group, Davis, Hughes, Sen. Javits, and a local NBC group, had to crawl on their hands and knees. It was slow-going and claustrophobic.

"As they approached the makeshift door, Martha Davis identified herself. 'I'm here with the people I told you about.' The area inside was only lighted by a couple of candles.

"Although the TV crew had been warned not to turn on its lights, they directed their bright lights into the dark room.

"During the midst of people screaming, 'Shit, turn that f … ing light off … what the f … is going on,' I got a glimpse of one guy sticking a needle into his arm and another sitting down getting ready to do the same thing. At that point, a fellow attempted to stab Hughes with a knife but missed. He was apprehended by an undercover New York City police officer assigned to the group. The entourage hurriedly exited the room and crawled through the tunnel back to the street.

"Back at the hotel Hughes called the mayor and insisted he release the young attacker. 'We were intruding on his territory,' said Hughes. The man was released.

"After our brief walk, we were escorted by Mrs. Davis to the Harlem Hospital, where she had taken over an entire floor to get the doctors to treat young addicts. Martha complained she received very little help from the medical establishment because of the stigma of heroin addiction. She was critical of some of the Black doctors who also refused to get 'involved' with 'those' patients. She also complained, as we were making our way to the heroin ward, that these children needed such things as toilet paper and other basic necessities.

"Senator Hughes started a dialogue with girls ten, eleven, and twelve, along with teenagers, who were trying to get off heroin. Some of them had been turned into addicts by their own mother, in order to prostitute them in securing more money for their own habit."[3]

"With amazing sensitivity, Hughes toured some of the more established detoxification programs set up in other areas of Harlem."

Bob Kholos continues, "In one such group, a woman paraded a group of young addicts, black and white, before us. They all had colorful uniforms and sang a couple of songs. The senator was not impressed because he felt they were too regimented and would have recurring problems once they got back into the real world with real pushers in their old neighborhoods.

"Hughes was taking this situation step by step. He identified with the addicts. He turned to me in almost a whisper and said, 'If the situation were reversed and I was now their age, instead of being an alcoholic, I would probably be a heroin addict.'"[4]

Bob continues, "Perhaps he would have been one of the glorified ten percent who recover from addiction and are able to go on with somewhat normal lives. But he became an alcoholic in his adult years, and as an adult was able to make the changes necessary to quit drinking for twenty years. If he had been an alcoholic at the age of nine, as some of these kids who were heroin addicts, I doubt that he would have become a productive member of our society.[5] With empathetic fervor, the senator toured another facility."

In January 1971 there was a ground swell of interest in the 1972 election. Many in the Democratic Party urged Hughes to run for president.

Notes

1 Kholos, Bob, "Sen. Harold E. Hughes — Last of the Great Democrats," an article used by permission from Pam Yeaton.
2 Ibid.
3 Ibid.
4 Ibid.
5 Ibid.

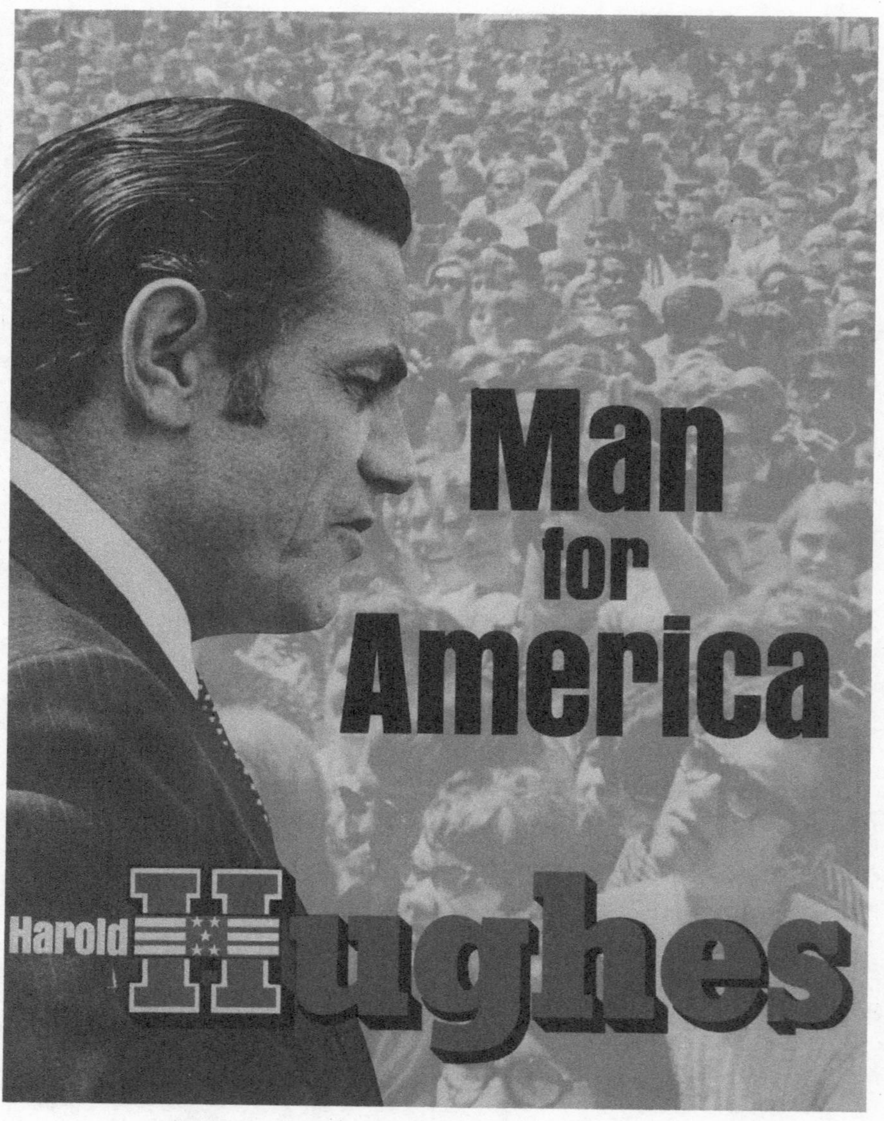

In January 1971 there was a ground swell of interest in the 1972 election and the Hughes Committee geared up. Many in the Democratic Party urged Hughes to run for president, although he eventually decided against running.
Photo: Cover of an informational brochure produced by The Hughes Committee.
Used with permission of the Hughes family.

CHAPTER TWENTY-FIVE

To Run or Not to Run for President?

Hughes' standing in the senate and in the country had grown exponentially. His views on the [Vietnam] war, now closely paralleled those of the Senate's most outspoken doves … Liberals outside of Washington increasingly are turning to Hughes for new leadership. He was sought out last year by a group of Liberal business and professional men from New York who developed the Fund for New Priorities in America, with the objective of reducing the role of the military and shifting government spending to domestic problems.[1]

NICK KOTZ AND JAMES RISSER

"The Democratic National Convention was to be held in Chicago in '68. Prior to the convention, liberals supporting Robert Kennedy and Eugene McCarthy found 'barriers built into the convention delegate selection process,' which convinced them that 'broad changes were imperative.' An ad hoc committee was created to discuss the selection process and report to the Rules Committee at the National Convention. Several prominent Democrats were asked to head the committee. All said no. Harold Hughes had not endorsed any candidate at that point, and he finally agreed to chair the committee. He worked learning the issues. The ad hoc committee issued a minority report to the Rules Committee of the Convention. The aim of the report was to make the Democratic Party more democratic. Hughes lobbied for passage of the report. He talked with Mayor Richard Daley and fellow Democratic governors urging passage. The minority report passed by 103 votes."[2]

A product of the minority report of the ad hoc committee was the appointment of the McGovern Commission. Harold Hughes participated in seminars and hearings throughout the nation. The hearings were completed, and the staff developed guidelines for changes in the delegate selection procedure.[3]

"A move surfaced to close the final meetings to press and public. Hughes said he would not take part if that were done. They were kept open."[3] During the commission's deliberations, it wrangled tediously for hours over key but complex guidelines. Mid-afternoon, the gavel was handed to Hughes, and in a brief statement he sorted out the issues and got a vote taken within the hour on every item that had been under discussion since early morning."[4]

"Harold Hughes gave the nomination speech for Senator Eugene McCarthy at the 1968 Democratic Convention in Chicago. The convention was a time of turmoil between the elements wanting an end to the war in Vietnam, and those, including Hubert Humphrey, supporting President Johnson's war policies. It was a difficult and turbulent time in the nation and in the Democratic Party, and it was felt by Hughes. He was running for a seat in the United States Senate and campaigning in a tough race. He later commented, 'My endorsement of Gene McCarthy in the midst of the campaign year, the death of Robert Kennedy, and the struggle for the reform of the party all impacted me. I took on some of the most bitter problems of party structure between conservative, liberal, hawks, and dove issues in our state that had ever been taken on, all in the same year.'"[5]

Hughes' work on the ad hoc committee, the McGovern Commission, and the nomination of Gene McCarthy brought him to the attention of young progressives, the doves, and the party reformers. As a result, the talk of Harold Hughes as a possible candidate for president began.

In 1970, the presidential election of 1972 was on the minds of a lot of people. Many of them wanted Senator Hughes to run for president. Democratic leaders in the Senate supported him. Joe Rosenfield, a Des Moines businessman and close friend and financial advisor of Hughes, Bill Knapp, another close friend and supporter of Hughes, and Warren Buffett took Hughes to New York City to introduce him to a group of Jewish financial leaders to test the financial waters. Bill Knapp remembers that Hughes told the group there would be no blank check for Israel if he were president. Later, Knapp asked Hughes, "Why the hell did you say that?"[6] But that approach was typical Harold Hughes. He said what he believed regardless of the circumstances and political fallout. Kotz and Risser wrote this about Hughes and the 1972 run for the thirty-sixth presidency: "Harold Hughes is a man on a mission. He is running for president not in the sense of an announced candidate or even as an active behind-the-scenes political maneuverer, but more in the manner of a man who feels some sort of distant calling and is getting ready. His inner feelings and his acute political senses tell him that the issues he is concentrating on are the vital ones in American society and ones on which a political future can be built. He knows the chance is remote that any call will come in 1972, and he is maintaining the low visibility that is sensible now. A staff member says that Hughes is available if the lightning strikes and acknowledges that he is moving toward a spot where the chances of lightning's striking are best.

"Perhaps unconsciously, the presidency was on his mind as Hughes walked with a sense of quiet exhilaration last November among the thousands of youth gathered at the Washington Monument to protest the war. He said that the peace movement is a living force, which will again gain strength, as there is new disenchantment with the war. And then he mused: 'In 1972, these kids who are eighteen now will be old enough to vote.' [Hughes' youngest daughter, Phyllis, told the authors of this book that she was actually in that crowd of protestors that day with a group of kids from her high school, only a few of whom knew he was her father.]

"Most of the time, one accepts Hughes' explanation that he is simply working on the issues he believes in, with no conscious aim toward a new political future. But at that point, one has momentarily forgotten that Harold Hughes, the sensitive human being, is also very much the astute and shrewd politician. That subtle blend has been his success, and it will determine in large measure where he goes from here."[7]

Hughes' standing in the Senate and in the country had grown exponentially. "His views on the [Vietnam] war, now closely paralleled those of the Senate's most outspoken "doves"[8] … Liberals outside of Washington increasingly are turning to Hughes for new leadership. He was sought out last year by a group of liberal business and professional men from New York who developed the Fund for New Priorities in America, with the objective of reducing the role of the military and shifting government spending to domestic problems."[9]

As this book is going to press, the United States administration is rattling the sword with Iran. This is a good time to emphasize that Senator Hughes was not only opposed to the Vietnam War but also was opposed to all war. In an article written by Nick Kotz and James Risser, they wrote, "He [Hughes] says, 'war is useless as a political instrument. I hate war, all war. Humanity itself is at stake.'"[10]

"Hughes traveled around the country speaking to political gatherings and on college campuses. He found support among these groups. His message stressed ending the war in Vietnam and he advocated finding ways to change the inequality and injustice that had resulted in racial crises. He believed the nation was in need of healing, and he strongly believed he possessed the qualities of leadership to bring healing about."[11]

"A trip was planned for Hughes to travel to several states. When informed that four of the top national journalists were invited to join Hughes on the trip, he wanted to cancel the trip. He remembered that George Romney's presidential run for the Republican nomination in 1968 ended when Romney said he had been 'brainwashed' on Vietnam. Hughes was fearful of a similar misstep with journalists on this trip. Once the staff convinced him to proceed, the trip was very successful. After a lengthy interview with Hughes, R.W. Apple of the *New York Times* said, "Seldom in my career have I met anyone as impressive as Hughes."[12]

"There were issues and concerns about Hughes' readiness to be president. Even though he was a member of the Armed Services Committee, he lacked experience in foreign affairs. He was a governor from a small state and his religious beliefs and spirituality concerned some people. These were matters raised by some letter writers to the senator. Others wrote of his compassion for people and that he was a rare person in politics."[13]

As interest grew in Hughes running for the nomination of president, Elizabeth Drew interviewed him on public television on February 9, 1971. She said, "From what I read, you might be going into another period of what you call fantastic change in your life. I don't really expect people to declare their candidacies on this program, although if you'd like to we'll give you time. But – would you like to?

SENATOR HUGHES: Not really, Liz.

MISS DREW: Okay. All right, that's fine. But short of that, and we all know, you are. "Dark horse" usually appears before or after your name, and you seem to have done one of those things that people seriously interested and thinking about running now do. You take a separate office somewhere in Washington, and a small staff goes to work. Would you tell us just what your thinking is on that? What you're thinking about doing?

SENATOR HUGHES: "Well basically, Liz, it's this. I had not considered the possibility of ever becoming even a presidential potential when I came to Washington two years ago. However, finding the turmoil that existed in the Democratic Party, plus my own interest in, and dedication to political party reform encouraged me to do more. My involvement in party reform, and my commitment generally to the great problems that our nation faces internationally and domestically, propelled the thought that we really had a void of any singular leadership in this Democratic Party, and there was a great deal of interest in my trying to assume that leadership. I reluctantly allowed some of it to move ahead.

"I say reluctantly, from the standpoint that I didn't view my chances, in all honesty, to be very good. I've restated some of my personal life, and the handicaps that it poses, naturally, and the curiosity that it brings. I have faced realistically the handicaps, in the fact that I am a new member of the United States Senate. I haven't been here twelve or fifteen years. I have been governor of my own state three times and elected to the senate and have a good political record, in my own state. But nationally I'm relatively unknown.

"A group of people wanted to start researching the idea, and I gave my full permission for them to do that, you know, to set up an outside operation to raise a small amount of money to continue that operation and to look the situation over to see whether the field was totally occluded from my being a candidate or not."[14]

"In an interview with reporters from the *Des Moines Register*, Hughes said he often sought the advice of his brother on difficult decisions. Reminded that his brother had been dead for years, Hughes replied, 'Yes, but I still talk to him [in personal contemplation].' Once the story circulated, it was a stunning blow to his possible run."[15]

Hughes thought about all the decisions he would face if he won the nomination and then the election. Nuclear threats, armaments, and relationships with communist countries would need a president's attention. He realized he could not push the red button in the case of a nuclear attack. He was seeing little of his family with all the traveling. He prayed about it and decided to end the effort. Hughes announced at a press conference on July 15.

Why did Hughes withdraw his name from the nomination of president? One reason Hughes gave was that he could not, in good conscience, press the button releasing a hydrogen bomb retaliating an attack on the U.S. At the same time that he made that decision he was seriously considering retiring from the Senate and engaging in lay ministry.

Another possible factor was that he was not well known. No doubt he knew his run for president would be a real challenge.

Another factor was his wife, Eva's mental health. Her illness was well known and it would have been difficult, if not impossible, to conduct a campaign for presidency and to take care of her at the same time. In an interview, the authors asked their daughter, Phyllis, "Do you think your mother's mental illness influenced your father's decision to not run for the presidency in 1972?"

She responded, "I think that's the main reason. I think there were other factors, of course. People were bringing up the spiritualism thing, because he never made a secret of studying it. Although, he eventually left that behind, my mother continued in it. People were questioning that, understandably. That was an issue, but I do think it could have easily been sort of put to bed. I do think the main reason he didn't run for president was her instability. The campaign would have been terrible for her, all the reports and the scrutiny and the campaigning. She was just too fragile and unstable."[16]

Perhaps the final blow was that the media picked up on Hughes' admission that he had communicated with his deceased brother, Jesse, in times of great stress. If the other factors had not closed the door on his aspirations, the public acknowledgement of contact with his brother would have made the decision for him.

Hughes summed it up as follows, "To continue the race for the presidency I would have to make many compromises. Yet I knew I couldn't do that to get greater financial and political support. If I did, I would lose my soul with every step I took down that road."[17]

The senator made the decision not to run for president. He also made another decision that shocked a lot of people and caused others in particular to think that he had lost his mind.

Notes

1 Kotz, Nick, and Risser, James, "Messiah from the Midwest?," *The Washington Monthly*, May 1970.
2 Wieck, Paul R., "The Presidential Candidacy of Harold Hughes, For God and Country," *The New Republic*, Reprinted by Permission. Copyright 1971 by Harrison-Blaine of New Jersey.
3 Ibid.
4 Ibid.
5 From recordings made by Harold Hughes in anticipation of his writing a book.
6 From an interview with William Knapp, Des Moines businessman, and friend and supporter of Hughes.
7 Kotz, Nick, and Risser, James, "Messiah from the Midwest?," *The Washington Monthly*, May 1970.
8 Ibid.
9 Ibid.
10 Ibid.
11 Wieck, Paul R., "The Presidential Candidacy of Harold Hughes, For God and Country," *The New Republic*, Reprinted by Permission. Copyright 1971 by Harrison-Blaine of New Jersey.

12 Metrovich, George, "Ida Grove Giant Left Many Impressions," Scripps Howard Foundation, 1996.

13 Hughes, Harold E., University of Iowa Library, Special Collections Division, Iowa City, Iowa.

14 Drew, Elizabeth, "Thirty Minutes with Harold Hughes," a television interview, WETA Public Broadcasting, Washington,D.C., February 9, 1971.

15 *Des Moines Register*, Iowa, October 27, 1996.

16 Comments by Phyllis Hughes Ewing, Harold Hughes' youngest daughter.

17 *Des Moines Register*, "Hughes' Story," personal selection, March 11, 1979.

Hughes enjoying his favorite pastime in 1970 during his tenure as U.S. Senator.
Photo: Personal family photo used with permission of the Hughes family.

CHAPTER TWENTY-SIX

A Momentous Decision — To Retire from the Senate

Some men, particularly politicians, will do almost anything for power. And then, having acquired it, they will do even more to consolidate and perpetuate it. For political power in the American way of life is either the ultimate money-substitute or an eased road to wealth. Once in a rare while, however, a man, elected to political power, decides to relinquish it when he doesn't have to.[1]

LLOYD SHEARER

In Senator Hughes' recorded words, "Doug [Halverson, a friend and brother from senate prayer breakfasts] was persistent. After every Wednesday prayer breakfast, he came by my office. He was the first person while I was in office who ever asked me to pray. I'd asked people before, but no one had asked me. Dick became my spiritual teacher and had much to do with my coming to understand Christ's love and acceptance.

"Since that day in my bathroom in 1954 when I bowed my knee to God, I've desired to follow him with all my heart. I've tried to find God in AA, in church activities, and doing good works. I got involved in the occult at one time in my life seeking greater truth. In all these places, I've hungered to find a deeper faith. Not all my experiences have been positive. There are practices among religious people in our land that nearly drove me away from God. It's only been in the past two years that I can honestly say that I've come to know Jesus Christ personally as my Savior, my Friend, and my Lord. Up to this time I've had numerous spiritual experiences, but never a personal encounter with Jesus Christ through His Holy Spirit. But now thanks to my daughter Carol, Eva, and brothers like Doug and Dick, I've gradually come to a deep commitment to Jesus Christ, and it has caused some significant changes in my life. The most significant has never been published. That is the love, forgiveness, and acceptance I found possible in Christ. And the new ways I'm learning to deal with my own pride.

"These changes have more personal significance than the decision I made in September, 1973, to leave my post in the Senate. Since 1954 when I quit drinking, I've thought of serving God in some 'full-time ministry.' I remember several discussions with Eva during the 50s when I shared my desire to become a missionary or a minister. I even took a correspondence course in preparation for the ministry.

"So when I had made my announcement that I would not run for reelection but would devote my time to ministering to man's spiritual needs, it was no new thought. It's not that I've been unhappy with the contributions I've made in the Senate. Actually, I'm quite proud about what I've been able to do in the fields of alcoholism, drug dependency, and the exposing of secret bombings. But I've searched for a way that I could do what God intended me to do with a total commitment. And I have not found that in the Senate.

"The truth is I've been sitting here in the Senate these recent years saying to myself I'm not doing what my conscience wants me to do. I'm not saying for a moment that politics is not important. But for me I am convinced that what is most important is a personal experience with Jesus Christ which will lead men and women to realize their first objective is to serve God. Serving God through politics and the social order is not enough for me. I've been in office for fifteen years. If I ran again for the Senate, another six years would reduce the time I would have left to devote my energies to leading others to Christ. It's not that I believe that I could not do God's work in the Senate, and rise to a place of power in the annals of our nation where I could change many things that I now feel need changing.

"But there is something more important than the structure of government on earth —more important than even the office of President. That is doing what God intends for you to do. To love

God with all your heart and soul and strength — 'seeking first the kingdom of God and His righteousness — that's important. Being faithful to my wife and family, friends and associates and my God. That's important too.'"[2]

On Wednesday, September 5, 1973, Senator Hughes called a press conference at which he made this statement: "I have called this press conference to announce a decision I have reached after a long period of personal soul-searching and extended discussion with the members of my family.

"The decision is this: When my present term as a United States Senator is ended, I will retire from the Senate and enter another field of public endeavor.

"Specifically, I will take up work as a religious lay worker in connection with two foundations — the Fellowship Foundation of Washington, D.C., and the International Christian Leadership.

"This new work represents to me a new kind of challenge and spiritual opportunity in today's troubled world. It is the kind of move I have long been motivated to take for profoundly personal religious reasons. As some who know me well will recall, I came very near leaving the business world for the ministry in the early 1950s. I have long been a lay speaker in the Methodist Church.

"Needless to say, only the most compelling individual commitment could persuade me to take leave of my work in government at a time when I am still in my most productive years and my faith in the causes we have labored for together remains undimmed.

"The hardest part of this is my sorrow at taking leave of friends and colleagues and the great association with thousands of other good Iowa citizens who I may not have known personally but always knew were there."[3]

The senator continued, "No words can describe the deep love and gratitude I feel for the people who have believed in me as a public official through the years — associates, supporters, citizens of all political faiths whom it has been my privilege to serve. These have been good years for me and my family — four years as Commerce

Commissioner, three terms as governor, and now a six-year term as United States senator."[4]

"If Hughes had remained in the Senate," said Kotz and Risser, "he would have been a shoe-in for election for another term. He would have gained financial security for himself and his wife, but he decided to retire."[5]

In that regard, Lloyd Shearer commented: "Some men, particularly politicians, will do almost anything for power. And then, having acquired it, they will do even more to consolidate and perpetuate it. For political power in the American way of life is either the ultimate money-substitute or an eased road to wealth.

"Once in a rare while, however, a man elected to political power, decides to relinquish it when he doesn't have to. Hughes is an exception. On September 5, 1973, he announced that he would not run again for the Senate. And that he did not plan to run for any other office.[6]

"The reaction to Hughes' plan [to leave the Senate] has been startling. The overwhelming response has been one of dissuasion. 'The devil's in the White House,' many of his constituents have written, 'stay in the Senate.' The secretaries in the senator's office say his Iowa mail has reflected surprise, disappointment, respect for his wishes, and appreciation for what he has done in the past, in that order. 'The only people who dislike the senator,' claims one assistant, 'are some in the White House, and that's because the senator has always firmly believed in telling people the truth and in speaking his own mind."[7]

The senator described his lay ministry as counseling and advising with senators and other government officials and through the sponsorship of prayer breakfasts and luncheons. He also included his work with prison inmates through the Prison Fellowship Ministry directed by Watergate personality Charles Colson.

According to Larry Johnson with the *Fairfield Ledger*, "These are private meetings with troubled senators at prayer luncheons attended by a few public officials. Politicians appear to be attracted to Hughes as if seeking some sort of redemption through embracing a man who has rejected the life many of them lead."

Hughes understands their troubles. 'I've stood in the limelight,' said the man who once briefly sought a presidential nomination. 'Believe me, the rewards are empty.'

The remainder of Hughes' ministry is carried out through the Assisi Foundation, which he describes as "simply the legal vehicle of my ministry." The Assisi Foundation includes two 'street ministries' in Washington, D.C., work at a Black prison there, and the lectures on alcohol and drug addiction."[8]

"An arm of Hughes' 'prayer warfare' is the National Prayer Breakfast, attended by top national officials each January or February, plus several similar, smaller groups."[9]

"Hughes said, "I'm just a layman serving Christ. That's what we all are. I may do it a little differently than you. If you truly want to serve, it requires an openness, a vulnerability to let God mold you into what he wants, whatever that may be. If you're committed, you will begin to pray for your leaders, beginning with those right here. Then we may one day become a nation under God."[10]

The *Des Moines Register* explains, "Hughes' dream is to establish a meeting place in the nation's capital where people from throughout the country and the world can go to pray together."[11]

The article continues, "Everywhere he, Hughes, goes on Capitol Hill, he is greeted warmly by the elevator operators, security guards, cleaning women, waitresses, and the scores of congressional staff assistants who know him or worked for him."[12]

Hughes returned to Iowa in 1981. During the 1980s he established several treatment centers, including a women's treatment program at Des Moines General Hospital in Des Moines and programs in Monticello and Mount Ayr, Iowa. The programs have closed, due largely to the effects of managed care, he maintained. Although the Hughes organization no longer owns or operates the centers, it is involved in weekend educational programs for people convicted of drunk driving.

"Hence, the mission of Harold Hughes through prayer breakfasts, through his continuing association with the Fellowship Foundation and with International Christian Leadership, through meetings at his Cedar Point Farm — is to listen, to be as Nick Carraway said of himself in Fitzgerald's Gatsby, "privy to the secret griefs of wild, unknown men," to hear God's footsteps in the world. "Wherever the need is, I go," Hughes says. "Sometimes it's accidental; I just run into men who want to talk, who want to see me. They may call and say, 'When are you coming to town? Would you stop in? I want to discuss something with you.' The people in Washington have accepted me now. My track record since retirement has given them the confidence to know that I'm not trying to run or betray anything they might share with me in another political party."[13]

Hughes re-appeared on the national scene again in the late 1980s when he took on the challenge of organizing the millions of Americans who had experienced recovery from alcoholism and other addictions. Hughes believed that people in recovery could go beyond their own personal recovery program and act as individual citizens.

As to why Hughes retired from the Senate, the first reason he gave was to engage full-time in a lay ministry. As he recorded, … "to do what my conscious wants me to do." And, the senator did just that. He retired from the Senate and moved with his wife and daughter, Phyllis, to Cedar Point, a twenty-one-acre compound and farm beside the water, near Royal Oak, halfway between St. Michaels and Easton on Maryland's Eastern Shore. When the crabs are running, they pull in half a bushel a day from the pots hung off the end of the dock stretching into the mouth of Broad Creek.[14]

Hughes gave up so much when he retired from the Senate that some people in Washington thought he had lost his mind. They thought he was not dealing with reality. And some people, including Les Holland, one of his staff that knew him best and traveled with him extensively, believes he was greatly influenced by his friend, Doug Coe. Coe was instrumental in organizing the Senate prayer breakfasts and spent a lot of time with the Senator. Les Holland and others believe that Coe, motivated by Republican associates, used his influence to persuade Hughes to drop out of the Senate and engage in lay ministry. As a result, that would get him out of the Senate and derail his potential for running for president.

Hughes joined his Ida Grove friend, Tubby Jacobson, and his wife, Ona Lee, at a café in Ida Grove in October of 1969. "I'm getting out of politics, Tubby," Hughes told Jacobson, "because I am fed up with them."[15] Hughes was an active person all of his life. He was active as a hunter and trapper as a boy, as a football player, a tuba player, and a singer in several groups. He was a very active person as the organizer of the Iowa Better Trucking Bureau. His activity as governor is historic. Perhaps the snail-pace of the Senate was not satisfying to the senator.

His age and the fact that he had been in politics for twenty years may have been another factor. He was very pro-active and engaged during most of those years. He was personally very active as governor of Iowa. As senator, he worked hard and was quite involved in alcoholism and addiction legislation and programming. In his political career he made hundreds of speeches all over the country. He was in his seventies. Perhaps he was just running out of steam.

Russ Wilson recalls a conversation with the senator in which he disclosed another possible reason he chose not to run for president. "It would take seven or eight million dollars to run and the only way I could raise that kind of money is by selling my soul. I'm not willing to do that." What a change from the millions of dollars that are spent on campaigns today.

Notes

1 Shearer, Lloyd, Senator Harold Hughes — "God's Work Comes First," *The Washington Post*, October 28, 1973.

2 From recordings made by Harold Hughes in anticipation of his writing a book.

3 Dateline Washington, D.C., A Report to Iowa, Senate Office Building, Washington, D.C., September 1973.

4 Ibid.

5 Kotz, Nick, and Risser, James, "Messiah from the Midwest?," *The Washington Monthly*, May 1970.

6 Shearer, Lloyd, Senator Harold Hughes — "God's Work Comes First," *The Washington Post*, October 28, 1973.
7 Johnson, Larry, "'Prayer Warfare' the Answer, Hughes Tells 850," *Fairfield Ledger*, July 26, 1980.
8 Ibid.
9 Ibid.
10 *Des Moines Register*, October 19, 1975
11 Ibid.
12 Kotz, Nick, and Risser, James, "Messiah from the Midwest?," *The Washington Monthly*, May 1970.
13 Means, Howard, "The Prophet." *The Washington Magazine*, Washington, D.C, July 1979
14 Ibid.
15 Article, "Hughes," *Des Moines Register*, Saturday, October 26, 1996.

Harold Hughes spent the final years of his life in Arizona with second wife, Julianne. Phyllis, Hughes' youngest daughter, credits Julianne with adding ten years to her father's life by helping him live a healthier lifestyle. Phyllis was especially appreciative that this time offered her young son, Jack, the opportunity to get to know his grandfather and build a relationship with him before he died. Photo: Personal family photo used with permission of the Hughes family.

CHAPTER TWENTY-SEVEN

Julianne and Harold in the Desert

In the fall of '87 the whole family moved to Arizona.
Wife, kids, dogs, horses, and goats.

JACQUIE HOLM-SMITH

In 1987 the senator divorced his wife, Eva, and later that year, married his former secretary, Julianne Holm, whose introduction to, and association with the Hughes' enterprise is interesting. Julie, as she was known, grew up in Fort Dodge, Iowa. Her grandmother, Vera Mattic, an active Democrat, got Julie interested in politics as a child.

When Julie's first husband, Lennis Holm, was accepted at Georgetown Law School in Washington, D.C., the couple moved to Washington. In the summer of 1970 Julie went to work on the Hughes Iowa Presidential Campaign. When that effort collapsed, she went to work in the senator's office.

As Ginger Roberts wrote in the *Fort Dodge Messenger*: "There she [Julianne] worked amidst the hoopla and hustle of the U.S. Senate, meeting "the big names" of politics, seeing the front-page news parade by before her eyes. Hundreds of people came through the office, lobbyists, students, presidential hopefuls, demonstrators, tourists, reporters, and people from all over. And when the people didn't come to her, she had the opportunity to go to them — Senate hearings, Congressional parties, political fundraisers, and rallies. She especially remembers the time she went to a fundraiser at the Kennedy home in Virginia, meeting Robert Kennedy's children, and other luminaries.

"'It was all a tremendous experience,'" she says, "'just incredible.'

"As for Hughes, she considers him 'the major political force in Iowa.'

"'He initiated a lot of reforms ... and people trust him because he's so honest. Iowa is traditionally Republican but there are a lot of Independents who go for the man, not the party.'

"She also thinks of Hughes as a very human person, citing the time he and his family flew out to Iowa for a vacation and took the Holms' twin daughters age three, along. On the flight out, the senator told stories and played games with them, then bought them candy during the layover at O'Hare Airport.

"As for the rest of Hughes' staff, he is known around Capitol Hill as being one of the warmest and friendliest, a reputation that Julie credits to administrative assistant, Park Rinard. "He treats the whole staff like they were members of a family," she explains. "And to him they really are."[1]

A romance developed between Hughes and Julianne and in 1987 they were married.

When he married Julianne, he not only gained a wife who shared his life with him until he died, but he also gained three stepchildren. Those additions were the twins, Jacquie and Jennifer, and a stepson, Hans Christian. The family lived in Iowa for a few years. And, as Jacquie wrote, "In the fall of '87 the whole family moved to Arizona; wife, kids, dogs, horses, and goats."

Hughes and Julie worked in the field of addiction, managed the treatment centers in Iowa, and traveled on his speaking circuit from 1989–1992. Jacquie and Jennifer worked from time to time with the Hughes treatment centers.

Phyllis Hughes Ewing recorded this story: "Early in their marriage, my dad, who battled with his weight most of his life, went to a "fat farm" in North Carolina. His plan was to stay for two weeks.

"After giving my dad a complete physical, the physician said, 'While you're here you've got to stop smoking, too.' My dad, a life-long addict sort of bristled and said, 'Well, I didn't agree to that. That's not what I came here for.'

"The doctor said, 'Look, I just gave you a physical. You're in the early stages of emphysema. If you don't quit smoking now, you're going to die in two years. If you're going to be dead in two years, why are you bothering to lose weight? Just go home, smoke, eat and die.'"

Phyllis continued, "My dad got his temper up, stomped out of the office, went back to his room, and was packing to go home. Julie talked him down as he tucked his tail between his legs and went back to the doctor. 'Okay, I'll try.' That's when he quit. Emphysema eventually would kill him but it would have killed him a decade sooner if he hadn't quit right then." Phyllis credits Julianne with adding that ten years to his life by helping him live a healthier lifestyle. Phyllis was especially appreciative that this time offered her young son, Jack, the opportunity to build a relationship with his grandfather before he died.

The couple eventually settled in Phoenix, Arizona. In a copy of a letter to a friend in Spain, dated January 21, 1996, Hughes wrote: "We are now at home at our residence called Desert Sands in Glendale, Arizona. We love it here in the desert, especially in the winter. Julianne still enjoys playing tennis and hiking. I'm rather disabled with asthma and emphysema. My athletic days are history, as are my political days. I'll be 74 years old on February 10, and together we are writing another book on my life. It has kept us quite busy. I'm considering the title of W.A.R.P. It's an acronym for Women, Alcohol, Religion, and Politics. It will be sort of a public confession and quite shocking to many people. I hope to complete it this year. My fishing and hunting days are pretty much behind me. I did go to Alaska salmon fishing in June of '93. My stepson accompanied me. It was one hell of a good time."

Hughes wrote, "I just received a clip through the mail from a friend in Iowa for my forty third anniversary in AA. I no longer go to meetings. The University of Wisconsin has named an education center in my honor called The Harold E. Hughes Center on Rural Issues. I was quite pleased by their honoring me in this way, since my own University of Iowa has more or less ignored me all of my life.

"At this point I thank God for each day of my life and do what I can to make it worthwhile to myself and others. My traveling is restricted because I'm unable to fly because of the effect on my lungs. I miss traveling."[2]

In a telephone interview [soon after he died in 1996,] his widow, Julianne, said that his health began to deteriorate about eighteen months [before]. Despite poor health, Hughes remained interested in public affairs. He had already cast an absentee ballot in the next month's election. He also maintained phone and fax contact with congressional leaders. "His body had weakened, but his voice was as strong as ever," she said.[3]

According to the account in a *Des Moines Register* October 25, 1996 retrospective, Harold and Julianne went on a picnic on Wednesday, October 23. When they returned home, he decided to take a nap. She discovered later in the evening that he had died in his sleep."[4]

As the senator's health declined, his finances were becoming critical as well. "In a gravelly voice, the seventy-five-year-old Democratic icon testified by telephone in July that 'It's a very humiliating, debilitating set of circumstances I find myself in.' He said he is 'going broke and confined to a wheelchair and dependent on oxygen tanks to breathe.' He petitioned the court for a decrease or elimination of his alimony payments to his former wife, Eva.'"

In spite of Hughes' failing health and financial challenges, the couple had many years of happiness together. They had many things in common which added to their lives. Jacquie Holm-Smith put it this way: "I hope the take-away on the Mom and Harold chapter is that they had a genuine love and a fabulous life. Health nut that she was, she no doubt extended his life. Those last few years when he could no longer travel and barely leave the house were hard, but they were two dynamic, delightful people up until the very end."

Following is a story that Hughes wrote about a pet bird that he acquired late in life while living in Arizona. It shows that in spite of his failing health and mounting financial challenges, he did not lose his sense of humor.

Sundown, The Bird

My wife, Julianne, recently gave me a beautiful bird. It was a bird that had been left with the mother of a ranch friend here in Arizona. This kind lady had developed a refuge for unwanted or troubled birds. As busy as she was working full time and maintaining a home, she had become concerned for birds that no longer were wanted. This one was a Jenday Conure, a small member of the parrot family, with a beautiful golden head, green wings, a rose colored breast and long blue grown tail feathers. The bird is a challenge!!

It seems the former owner and his wife had a problem with the bird. When the husband left for work in the morning, his wife didn't have time for the bird so she stuck it in a closet for the day until the husband came home. After five years of this, the little parrot had become very noisy, mean and ill tempered. So did the couple that was supposed to care for him and they got a divorce. The man got the bird and couldn't manage it alone, so he left it with his ex-wife Janis with the understanding that she would find it a good home. Since the bird didn't like women, Janis was looking for a man for the bird to live with. Now Janis had sixteen other birds so when my wife called inquiring about different birds that I might like (my wife was convinced that a bird would be a good companion for me on my down days), they decided that we would try this bird with the agreement that if it didn't work out we could return the bird.

When we met the bird, he immediately took to me, but since a woman had stuck him in a closet for five years, he wanted nothing to do with Julianne. We decided to take the bird and try it. We followed Janis home to look at the kind of cage we needed to buy and also to get about twenty-five bird magazines and some bird seed because she fed it a certain kind that could only be bought at a pet store that was closed for the evening. We then stopped at PetSmart and bought $250.00 worth of cages, toys, a bird playpen, and a book on conures. Now this seven-year-old mean little bird is on his way to live with a seventy-four-year-old man who is just as mean as he is. For some reason I can't quite understand, Julianne thought this would make us both happy. As near as I could tell, the only happy one in the place was Janis as she waved good-bye to me and that yellow-headed screaming little parrot. I was feeling okay about it because I figured within a week I'd take the blankety-blank bird back and tell her it didn't work out. That way Julianne would be happy, the bird would be no worse off and I could get on with grumping at my two huge mastiffs (130 and 200 pounds), who think they own the house I live in.

Tragedy strikes as Janis died unexpectedly at age fifty-seven.

Of course by now you have guessed that I can't take the bird back to the family of broken hearts. There are a number of spiritual questions raised by all of these events. Is it possible that God did cut off my last logical method of getting rid of this cantankerous love gift from the most wonderful lady in my life? Is it possible that God was upset with Janis and her mother for sponging for a week in a gambling resort and not gambling? Even worse, is it possible God is punishing the bird for his rotten attitude by forcing him to live with me for the rest of my life? Is it possible reincarnation really is a fact and Lyndon Johnson is finally getting even with me for pulling out in my support of him on Vietnam? The thoughts and possibilities are endless over this dilemma.

Anyway, six weeks have now passed and I have named the bird "Sundown." I really wanted to name him "Newt" after you know who, because he yells all the time and nothing he says makes any sense. I had limitless possibilities, but since the bird only says two words, he was no help at all. In fact, I don't even know if it is a she or a he and I don't have $100.00 to have it sexed. The problems just continue to mount. In the meantime, we are becoming more and more friendly. It actually is frightening to think that I'm stuck with disciplining this multi-colored bit of life that even St. Francis would have had a problem with. I'm getting concerned for both of us, because I think Sundown is making more progress than I am.

I have a Bible study three days a week with Julianne and her son, Hans. Julianne was brought up in the Catholic Church and Hans' father was a Lutheran who thought church was an extended arm of the business community. Julianne was more interested in reading books on the church's forbidden list than most other reading. The Bible was not something to worry about; the church took care of everything. Hans Christian grew up believing the Bible was a bookend because no one ever moved it. Anyway, on any given Monday, Wednesday, and Friday at 11 a.m. you can find the three of us, plus the bird, hovering over our Bibles searching with one another in the word of God. So far, the mastiffs sit quietly by and act as though they accepted the love years ago and have no worries whatever. Neither of them trust the bird and I know full well the bird does not love them, so the Lord has his work cut out for him because they all three close their eyes at one time, when we pray. I know because I keep one eye open myself just in case.

If you have read this far, I know you are a brother who loves blindly or has great concern for my mental health. According to the scientists and doctors I'm keeping supplied with vacation money, my brain is the only healthy thing in my whole body. That should tell you in one sentence that I'm standing in need of prayer.

Most of this story I wrote in the hope you would find in it a break from the ordinary, and along with me, enjoy the somewhat questionable return of my sense of humor. I hope it has accomplished its purpose.[5]

Hughes with Sundown, the bird he loved.
Photo: Personal family photo used with permission of the Hughes family.

Notes

1 Roberts, Ginger, "Julie Comes Back to Iowa," *Fort Dodge Messenger*, Thursday, December 21, 1972.

2 *Des Moines Register*, Tuesday, August 27, 1996.

3 *In Memoriam, Remembering Harold E Hughes*; https://www.well.com/user/woa/harolde.htm.

4 *Des Moines Register*, Tuesday, October 25, 1996.

5 From recordings made by Harold Hughes in anticipation of his writing a book.

CHAPTER TWENTY-EIGHT

A Tribute to a Quintessential Man

Notable tributes to Harold Hughes following his death in 1996

"The West lost two singularly resolute peacemakers with the death of former Senator Harold Hughes of Iowa and Magda Troeme of France. Both were pacifists by belief and action who put their lives at the service of people ignored by society. Both were innately modest about their work of rescue — alcoholics for Hughes and Jewish refugees for Troeme — and saw it as the most natural of responses."[1]
COLMAN MCCARTHY of the *Washington Post*, on the death of Harold Hughes

"When someone asked me to characterize Harold Hughes, I called him the quintessential Iowan ... He was the purest of his kind — his flaws even had a majesty — and he never tried to fool himself or pretend to be something he wasn't.

"In Iowa, virtually every aspect of government was modernized or set in motion for modernization by Hughes. The jewel is the community college system — 28 campuses teaching the equivalent of more than 60,000 full-time students."[2]

"Courtesy of Hughes, and policies continued and fine-tuned by his Republican successor, Robert Ray, and a host of legislators, Republicans and Democrats, Iowa government is basically a well-run, responsive machine. Not many states can make that claim."[3]
JAMES FLANSBURG, former *Des Moines Register* columnist

"Now with Harold Hughes gone, I shall prefer to think of him not as the man who ended his life amid a series of painful domestic problems, but as the subject of columnist Mary McGrory's exclamation to me, following a rousing Hughes speech to an audience of African-American

leaders in Chicago in 1972: 'My God', Mary said, 'that man looks and sounds like a real President.'"[4]
GEORGE ANTHAN, *Des Moines Register's* Washington D.C. Bureau Chief, in his recollections

"Hughes was a 'diamond in the rough' who became a multi-faceted man."[5]
JUSTICE BRUCE M. SNELL, JR., Iowa Supreme Court Justice

"I think Governor Hughes had an enormous influence on a whole generation of people in Iowa. John Kennedy in Washington and Harold Hughes in Des Moines — they were an inspiration to a generation. They thought that public service was important and rewarding for the people to be involved in."[6]
TOM MILLER, Iowa Attorney General

"Hughes was someone who you never forgot once you met him. When he walked into a room he had presence and everyone felt that. His powerful voice and size were attributes that helped him in his political career. Hughes' memory was exceptional. I think he had a photographic mind. He never forgot anything ... that was one of his great strengths. He was trustworthy beyond anyone I have ever known as well as the most honest man I have ever met."
BILL KNAPP of Des Moines, a close friend and longtime Hughes supporter

"[He was] the most telling and moving orator I've ever heard."[7]
JAMES FLANSBURG, former *Des Moines Register* columnist

"As a public speaker Hughes progressed from being painfully awkward to being able to mesmerize an audience. He was at home on a political stump, in a church pulpit, in an academic setting, or over a bean supper in a mission."[8]
GENE RAFFENSPERGER, former *Des Moines Register* staffer

"He was a very gifted person, and history will show he was a great leader for the state." [9]
GOVERNOR ROBERT RAY, former Iowa governor

"He walked where angels fear to tread, whether in the Legislature or with some poor soul who had no place to go."[10]
EDWARD CAMPBELL, longtime Hughes aide

"His greatest asset was his willingness to speak forthrightly on an issue regardless of the effect on his future. He didn't color them for his own political benefit."[11]
ROBERT D. FULTON, Governor Harold Hughes' Lieutenant Governor, 1965–1969

"He would want to be remembered most for his love of the people and state of Iowa, and for his fifty years of work to provide treatment and recovery for alcoholics and all other drug-addicted persons. He would have celebrated forty-three years of sobriety next year."[12]
PHYLLIS HUGHES EWING, Harold Hughes' youngest daughter

"[He was remembered as] a political colossus who remade state government in Iowa and left a legacy that still touches the lives of the state's residents ... the charismatic Hughes will go down in history as one of the state's greatest governors, friends, ... (He) decided what he thought was best and then used his impressive oratorical skills to shape public opinion. Even though people would disagree with them, they respected his courage."[13]
DAVID YEPSEN, former *Des Moines Register* staff

"On each occasion I was deeply impressed — with his eloquence, his personal bearing, his warmth, his obvious commitment to the cause we shared, and, yes, his deep, resonant voice, ("The Voice," we called him), which literally forced you to listen to what he had to say. I recall his gentle smile when I shared with him that my dad had been a small-time trucker for many years and certainly could have used his

advocacy when I was a kid. Certainly it is no exaggeration to say that Harold Hughes made a unique contribution to public policy and to the quality of life for all Americans. He inspired many with his leadership and example. As Senator Hughes passes from the scene, I can't help wondering whether his vision of a million people in recovery, united in advocacy of prevention and treatment, will ever be realized. And whether we will ever see such leadership in the halls of Congress again."[14]

THE A TEAM, Missouri Division of Alcohol and Drug Abuse

"A giant of a man died on October 23, 1996, at his home in Glendale, Arizona. He was a giant in more ways than one. The obituaries and tributes that appeared during the week following his death hardly grasp the meaning of his life for millions who have recovered, are recovering, and will recover from alcoholism and other drug addictions. Or for those who work in the field of prevention.

"The death of Harold Everett Hughes marks the passing of one of the true pioneers in the field of alcohol and other drug abuse. All who work in the field owe a debt of gratitude to Harold Hughes — both for his accomplishments and for his example. More than just a public figure, he has been described by friends and colleagues as 'a life force.' He was an extraordinary man with an extraordinary career." [15]

THE A TEAM, Missouri Division of Alcohol and Drug Abuse

After the Senator died, the publication, *Addiction*, published an article, *Conversation with Senator Harold Hughes*. The article included this tribute by Senator Edward Kennedy. Senator Kennedy was shown a copy of this interview with Senator Hughes and he very kindly provided the following comment for publication: "This eloquent interview with Harold Hughes reminds me of how much he accomplished in his extraordinary life and how much we missed him when he left the Senate. He was a powerful force for compassion and justice. His vigorous pursuit of fair treatment for persons battling addiction is legendary. He had approached his own problem with honesty and frankness, at a time when the rest of America discussed alcohol abuse in whispered tones, behind closed doors. Harold Hughes changed all that, and brought hope and help to vast numbers of his fellow citizens. The country continues to reap the benefits of his work, included in the establishment of the National Institute on Alcohol Abuse and Alcoholism at the National Institute of Health. If we see farther today on these important issues, it is because we stand on the shoulders of giants like Harold Hughes."[16]

Notes

1 McCarthy, Colman, "Two Lives of Peacemaking and Service,"*Washington Post*, November 12, 1996.
2 Flansburg, James "Faith in Democracy," *Des Moines Register*, November 3, 1996.
3 Ibid.
4 Anthan, George, "Harold Hughes: A Reporter's Recollections," *Des Moines Sunday Register*, October 1996.
5 Snell, Bruce, *Des Moines Register*, Sunday, November 16, 1996.
6 Miller, Tom, "Iowa Remembers Harold Hughes," *The Cedar Rapids Gazette*, October 25, 1996.
Knapp, William, in a conversation with the authors
7 Flansburg, James, *Des Moines Register*, October 25, 1996.
8 Raffensperger, Gene, *Des Moines Register*, October 25, 1996.
9 Ray, Governor Robert, *Des Moines Register*, October 25, 1996
10 Campbell, Edward, *Des Moines Register*, October 25, 1996.
11 Fulton, Lieutenant Governor Robert, *Des Moines Register*, October 25, 1996.
12 Ewing, Phyllis, *Des Moines Register*, October 25, 1996.
13 Yepsen, David, *Des Moines Register*, October 25, 1996.
14 In Memoriam, Remembering Harold E. Hughes, www.well.com/user/woa/harolde.htm, Adopted from an obituary by Gerrit DenHartog published in the "A" Team, Missouri Division of Alcohol and Drug Abuse.
15 Ibid.
16 "Conversation with Senator Harold Hughes," Journal Interview 39, *Addiction*, Washington D.C., 1997.

RUSSELL L. WILSON

Russell L. Wilson and Harold Hughes were close friends for many years. "He was like a brother to me," Wilson said. Their families remained friends throughout Hughes' life.

In 1962 when Hughes was governor, he appointed Wilson to the Iowa State Board of Control that administered thirteen state institutions including prisons, training schools for youth, mental hospitals, and several residential institutions. In the four years that Wilson served on that board he accompanied Hughes on several state and political trips and administered several special projects for the Governor including the Iowa Comprehensive Alcoholism Project.

Wilson, a retired clergyman, has co-authored two additional books and has published many articles. His personal contact with Hughes provides many insights into Hughes' career and life. He also shares many stories about Hughes that have never been published.

WILLIAM HEDLUND

William G. Hedlund graduated from Iowa State University in 1958 with a major in history and minors in government and industrial administration. He was employed by the Legislative Research Bureau from 1959 to 1962. He then returned to Iowa State to work on a masters degree.

In 1964, he took the opportunity to join the staff of Governor Harold Hughes. He was responsible for health/education, welfare, and revenue. He went on to serve on Senator Harold Hughes' staff as legislative assistant and office manager from 1969 to 1972.

After returning to Iowa, Hedlund owned a retail store for 13 years then managed two housing projects for the elderly.

APPENDIX I

Governor Harold E. Hughes' Recommendations Enacted by the Legislature

1963 Session of the Iowa Legislature

Liquor by the Drink
New Commercial Code
Public Utilities Rate-Regulation
Gave Municipalities a Greater Measure of Home Rule
Program to Combat Mental Retardation
Kerr-Mills Medicare Plan Funding
The Investment of Idle Public Funds

1965 Session of the Iowa Legislature

Proposed Constitutional Amendments

- Established Annual Sessions of the Legislature
- Item Veto for Governor on Appropriation Bills
- Rule for Municipalities
- Legalized Bingo for Charitable and Religious Organizations
- Authority for Governor to Appoint Some State Office Holders
- Extended the Terms of Governor and Lt. Governor from Two to Four Years and Run as a Team
- A Reapportionment Plan

Increased the Gas Tax
Established Four New Vocational-Technical Schools
Abolished Capital Punishment
New Water Pollution Control Program
Educational Scholarship Program for Young Iowans
Control of Billboards on the Highways
Withholding of State Income Tax
Repeal of Five of the Six-Mill Tax on Moneys and Credits
Mandatory Seat Belt Law
Reorganization of the State Board of Health
Comprehensive Drive Education Program
Industrial Safety Law
Establishment of the Higher Education Facilities Commission
New Alcoholic Treatment Facility
Funding for a Maximum Security Hospital
Enactment of the Intergovernmental Cooperation Act

Comprehensive Study of the Structure of State Government
Establishment of the State Civil Rights Commission

1967 Session of the Iowa Legislature
Proposed Constitutional Amendments Approved the Second Time
  Home Rule for Municipalities
  Item Veto for Governor on Appropriation Bills
Annual Sessions of the Legislature
  A Permanent Reapportionment Plan
A Statewide Television Network
Civil Service System for State Employees
Established and Funded Building for Peace Officers Academy
Humane Slaughtering of Livestock Law
Authorized State Aid to Local Communities Hit by Natural Disasters
Established State Arts Council
Conflict of Interest Regulation
Reorganization of Board of Control, Board of Social Welfare to One Department
Exemption of Amish Children Attending Public Schools from State Requirements
Established an Intermediate Security Prison

1963–1969 Administrative Implementations as Governor
Established the Oakdale Facility for Evaluation of Mentally Ill Inmates
Strengthened the Iowa Development Commission
Conducted "Sell Iowa Trips" in the U.S. and Missions to Europe, Mexico, South America, and the Orient
Created a State Crime Commission
Issued an Executive Order Forbidding Discrimination in Employment by State Agencies
Established a Statewide On-the-Job-Training Program

APPENDIX II

The Hughes Family's Personal Recollections of his Political Highlights

1990	Established SOAR Foundation, Inc.
1988	Appointed Trustee of the National Citizen's Committee on Alcoholism
1986	Keynoted the Second North American Congress on Alcoholism and Drug Problems
1984	Founded Harold Hughes Centers, Inc., Des Moines, Iowa
1978	Appointed by President Carter to Chair the National Commission on Alcoholism and Alcohol Related Problems
1976–78	Appointed by the United States Senate to serve as Chairman of the Committee on Operations of The United States Senate
1976	Chaired and keynoted the First North American Congress on Alcoholism and Drug Problems
1975–80	Consultant and worked for the Assisi Foundation of Washington, D.C.
1975–77	President of the World Congress on Alcoholism and Addictions
	Former member of the Board of Directors and the Advisory Board of The National Council on Alcoholism
1973	U.S. Senate representative in negotiations for control of psychotropic substances at the Vienna Treaty Conference
Spring 1972	Co-chaired Senator Edmund Muskie's presidential campaign
1971	Sought delegates for nomination for the office of President of the United States
1969–75	Served in the United States Senate
	Served on the Health and Human Services, Veterans Affairs, and Armed Services committees
	Chaired the first subcommittee in U.S. Senate history to deal with alcoholism and addiction
	Primary author of Public Law 96-616 "The Hughes Bill," which established the National Institute on Alcohol Abuse and Alcoholism (NIAAA)
1968	Elected to the U.S. Senate
1962–69	Served three two-year terms as Governor of Iowa

1964–69	Served on the Executive Committee for the National Governor's Conference
1965–69	Elected Chairman of the National Governors Caucus
1964	Gave seconding speech for nomination of Lyndon B. Johnson as president of the United States
1962	Elected Governor of Iowa
1958	Elected to the Iowa State Commerce Commission
1955	Founded the Iowa Better Trucking Bureau
1953–55	Field Representative for the Iowa Motor Truck Association
1947–52	Truck line manager
1942–45	U.S. Army

ACKNOWLEDGMENTS

Thank you to William (Bill) Knapp
for his support in the writing of this book and
for his generous financial support.

Thank you to friends, family, and colleagues
of Harold Hughes who shared their personal insights
and stories in this book.

Jeni Holm Cooper
Phyllis Hughes Ewing
Julianne Hughes
Gene Kieffer
William (Bill) Knapp
Jacquie Holm-Smith
Pam Yecton

Thank you for research assistance

Patrick Deluhrey
William (Bill) Gannon
Dwight Jensen
Bob Kholos
Jack Kibbie
Leo Landis and the staff, Iowa State Historical Library, Des Moines
The staff of the Special Collections, Library
of the University of Iowa, Iowa City

Typing, Editing and Proofreading,
Transcription, Technical Support

Barbara Briggie Smith
Diane Collett
Patrick Deluhrey
Sharyl Heiken
James Hufferd

Stacey Kimberlin
Michelle Riesenberg
Reverend Dr. David Stout
Connie Wilson
Kristin Wilson

Cover Design and Project Management
Connie Wilson

**To our wives,
who lived these memories with us and
supported this book's journey.**
Rosemary Hedlund
June Wilson